GRILLED COOKBOOK

Making More Memories in Your Kitchen With Grilled Steak Cookbook!

(An Inspiring Bbq and Grilling Cookbook for You)

Robert Parker

Published by Sharon Lohan

© Robert Parker

All Rights Reserved

Grilled Cookbook: Making More Memories in Your Kitchen With Grilled Steak Cookbook! (An Inspiring Bbq and Grilling Cookbook for You)

ISBN 978-1-990334-81-8

All rights reserved. No part of this guide may be reproduced in any form without permission in writing from the publisher except in the case of brief quotations embodied in critical articles or reviews.

Legal & Disclaimer

The information contained in this book is not designed to replace or take the place of any form of medicine or professional medical advice. The information in this book has been provided for educational and entertainment purposes only.

The information contained in this book has been compiled from sources deemed reliable, and it is accurate to the best of the Author's knowledge; however, the Author cannot guarantee its accuracy and validity and cannot be held liable for any errors or omissions. Changes are periodically made to this book. You must consult your doctor or get professional medical advice before using any of the suggested remedies, techniques, or information in this book.

Table of contents

Part 1 1
1. Goat Cheese Grilled Sandwiches with Fig and Honey 2
2. Cheddar & Cream Cheese Grilled Sandwiches with Jalapenos 4
3. Jarlsberg Cheese Grilled Sandwiches with Deli Ham 6
4. Brie Cheese Grilled Sandwiches with Tomato and Spinach . 8
5. Cream Cheese Grilled Sandwiches with Biscoff and banana 10
6. Provolone Cheese Grilled Sandwiches with Fried Egg 12
7. Mozzarella Cheese Grilled Sandwiches with Veggies 14
8. White Cheddar Cheese Grilled Sandwiches with Avocado & Tomatoes 16
9. Fontina Cheese Grilled Sandwiches with Honey & Basil 18
10. Goat Cheese Grilled Sandwiches with Bell Peppers & Portobello 20
11. Provolone Cheese Grilled Sandwiches with Sloppy Joes . 22
12. Cheddar Cheese Grilled Sandwiches with Green Apple 24
13. Mozzarella Cheese Grilled Sandwiches with Zucchini 25
14. 4 Cheese White pizza Grilled Sandwiches 27
15. Mozzarella, Cheddar & Cream Cheese Grilled Panini with Green Goddess salad 29
16. Provolone Cheese Grilled Sandwiches with Roast Beef and Caramelized Onion 31
17. Fontina Cheese Grilled Panini with Prosciutto Ham & Figs 33
18. Gruyere Surchoix Cheese Grilled Sandwiches with Toasted Almonds 34

19. Gruyere Cheese Grilled Sandwiches with Olives & Tomatoes 36

20. Colby Jack Cheese Grilled Sandwiches with Nachos 38

21. Macaroni & Cheese Grilled Sandwiches with Pulled Pork & Barbecue Sauce 40

22. Muenster Cheese Grilled Sandwiches with Ham & Spinach 42

23. Parmesan & Mozzarella Cheese Grilled Sandwiches with Spinach Artichoke dip 43

24. Cheddar Cheese Grilled Sandwiches with Piquillo peppers 45

25. Manchego Cheese Grilled Panini with Mushrooms & Shallots 47

26. Brie Cheese Grilled Sandwiches with Raspberries & Nutella 49

27. American Cheese Grilled Sandwiches with Cheese Sticks 50

28. Cheddar Cheese Grilled Sandwiches with Beef & Onions 51

29. Cheddar Cheese Grilled Sandwiches with Ham & Pineapple 53

30. Havarti & Cheddar Cheese Grilled Sandwiches with Garlic & Green Onion Mashed Potato 54

31. Cream Cheese Grilled Bagel Sandwiches 56

Part 2 58

Dialysis Cookbook DIALYSIS DIET COOKBOOK 59

BREAKFAST 59

1. Maple Sausage 60

Lemon-Blueberry Corn Muffins Yield: 12 Serving 62

Lemon Apple Honey Smoothie 64

Puffy Chili Rellenos Casserole	65
Mexican Brunch Eggs	67
Master Mix	69
40-Second Omelet	70
Apple Bran Muffins	71
Banana-Apple Smoothie	74
Banana Oat Shake	75
Chicken and Corn Chowder	76
Canned Fish Tacos	78
Beef Barley Soup	79
Chicken and Dumplings	81
Chicken N' Orange Salad Sandwich Yield: 6 Servings	83
Chinese Chicken Salad	84
Cider Cream Chicken	86
Cowboy Caviar Bean and Rice Salad Yield: 6 Servings	87
Fruity Chicken Salad	89
Low Salt Stir-Fry	91
Herb Breaded Chicken	93
Honey Herb Glazed Turkey	95
Hungarian Goulash	97
Italian Meatballs	99
Jammin' Jambalaya	100
Kickin' Chicken Tacos	103
Lamb Sirloin	105
Lemon Curry Chicken Salad	107
Louisiana BBQ Shrimp	108
Marinated Shrimp & Pasta Salad Yield: 10 Servings	110

- The King 112
- Veggie Grilled Cheese Sandwich 113
- Ham and Apple Grilled Cheese 114
- Jalapeno Popper Grilled Cheese Sandwich 116
- Grown Up Grilled Cheese Sandwich 118
- Sneaky Grilled Cheese Sandwich 120
- Ham and Broccoli Grilled Cheese 122
- Grilled cheese with apple and cinnamon 124
- Grilled Cheese with Tomato, Peppers and Basil 125
- Pepper jack, avocado, bacon sandwich 126
- Grilled Cheese with avocado and fruit glaze 127
- Dulce de Leche Grilled Cheese 129
- Cinnamon apple deluxe 130
- Pico De Gallo Grilled Cheese Sandwich 132
- Grilled Hawaiians 134
- SPAM, Tomato, Cheddar Cheese, and Sweet Onion Sandwiches 135
- Grilled Mushroom and Swiss 136
- Turkey and Feta Grilled Sandwich 138
- Brie and Pear Sandwich 139
- Turkey and swiss Sandwich 140
- Grilled Camembert Sandwich 141
- Roasted Red Pepper and Ham Sandwich 142
- Grilled Peanut Butter and Banana Sandwich 143
- Turkey Reuben Sandwiches 144
- Chicken Cordon Bleu Sandwich 145
- Amazing Whisky Grilled Baby Back Ribs Recipe 146

Baby Back Ribs with Espresso Barbecue Sauce 148

Baby Back Ribs with Spicy Peach BBQ Sauce 151

Baked BBQ Baby Back Ribs 153

Barbecue Chicken Recipe 155

Barbecue Ribs with Gochujang Sauce 157

Barbecue St. Louis Pork Ribs 160

Barbecued Chicken on the Grill 163

Barbecued Seitan Ribz (Vegan Ribs) 166

Barbecued Style Braised Short Ribs Recipe 168

BBQ Baby Back Ribs 170

BBQ Boneless Country Ribs 173

BBQ Pulled Pork Sandwiches 175

Best Barbecue Ribs Ever 177

Best Darn Instant Pot Boneless Pork Chops 179

Best-Ever Barbecued Ribs 182

Beth's Melt in Your Mouth Barbecue Ribs 184

Chipotle Barbecue Ribs 186

Fall-Off-The-Bone Oven Baked Ribs Recipe 188

Part 1

1. Goat Cheese Grilled Sandwiches with Fig and Honey

Preparation Time: 17 – 20 minutes
Cooking Time: 12 minutes
Ready In: 30 minutes
Servings: makes 4 sandwiches

INGREDIENTS:

2 teaspoons Honey
8 slices Cinnamon-Raisin bread
2 tablespoons Fig preserves
¼ teaspoon Grated lemon rind
1 (4-ounce) Packaged Goat Cheese
2 teaspoons thinly sliced Fresh basil
1 teaspoon Powdered Sugar for cooking spray

METHOD:

1. Take the honey, grated lemon rind and goat cheese in a bowl and stir them until they blend nicely into a mixture.
2. Spread a little of this mixture on 4 cinnamon-raisin bread slices and put 1 ½ teaspoons of fig preserves and ½ teaspoon of basil on each of these 4 slices.
3. Cover these ready slices with the remaining 4 slices of the bread and coat the outer surface of the bread lightly with cooking spray.

4. Place 2 sandwiches on a pan and press them gently with a cast-iron or heavy skillet on top to flatten.

5. Place the pan with the sandwiches in a large, nonstick pre-heated skillet set to medium heat and let the sandwiches cook for 3 minutes on each side or until the bread is lightly toasted (leave the cast-iron skillet on the sandwiches while they cook).

6. Repeat steps 4 and 5 with the remaining 2 sandwiches.

7. Sprinkle lightly with powdered sugar before serving.

2. Cheddar & Cream Cheese Grilled Sandwiches with Jalapenos

Preparation Time: 34 minutes
Cooking Time: 6 – 8 minutes
Ready In: 40 – 45 minutes
Servings: makes 1 sandwich

INGREDIENTS:

2 Jalapeno peppers, seeded and cut in half lengthwise
½ cup Jack and Cheddar Cheese, shredded
2 tablespoons Cream Cheese , room temperature
2 slices Sour dough bread
1 tablespoon Butter, room temperature
1 tablespoon Crumbled Tortilla chips

METHOD:

1. Arrange the jalapenos with the cut side facing down on a baking sheet.
2. Place this baking sheet in the oven (preferably on the top shelf) and broil for about 10-12 minutes until the outer layer of the jalapeno skin has blackened.
3. Seal the jalapenos in a zip-lock bag and let them cool until you can work with them.

4. After around 20 minutes, try to peel off the skin from the peppers, they will come off easily. Keep these peeled jalapenos aside.

5. Coat the outside of each slice of bread lightly with butter and spread the cream cheese on the inside.

6. Sprinkle half of the shredded cheese on top of the cream cheese. Add jalapenos, crumbled tortilla chips, and the remaining cheese on the top.

7. Finally place the other slice of bread on the top.

8. Heat a non-stick pan to medium heat.

9. Place the sandwich on the pan and put it in the oven to grill until the bread is golden brown. The cheese will melt after you've heated it for about 2-4 minutes per side. Serve hot!

3. Jarlsberg Cheese Grilled Sandwiches with Deli Ham

Preparation Time: 10 minutes
Cooking Time: 6 – 8 minutes
Ready In: 20 minutes
Servings: makes 1 sandwich

INGREDIENTS:

4 slices Jarlsberg cheese
1 Yellow Onion, separated into rings
2 slices Deli sliced ham
2 slices Italian style loaf bread
Butter, as required for cooking

METHOD:

1. Sauté the onion rings in about 1/4 tablespoon of butter over medium heat in a cast iron pan until their edges are slightly crispy. Remove from pan once done.
2. Spread a generous amount of butter on one side of each slice of bread.
3. On top of the non-buttered side of bread, place 2 slices of Jarlsberg cheese, 2 slices of Deli ham, the onions sauté-d earlier, and then the remaining 2 slices of cheese.
4. Place the other side of bread on top of the ham and cheese toppings with the butter side up.

5. Using about 1/2 tablespoon of butter, heat the sandwich in the pan on medium heat. Make sure the sandwich sizzles.

6. Let it cook for about 2 minutes on one side or until the side is a nice, golden brown and then flip the sandwich over.

7. Keep it on the pan until the cheese is melted and the bread turns to a nice, golden brown. Serve hot!

4. Brie Cheese Grilled Sandwiches with Tomato and Spinach

Preparation Time: 10 – 12 minutes
Cooking Time: 8 minutes
Ready In: 20 minutes
Servings: makes 4 sandwiches

INGREDIENTS:

4 ounces Brie cheese, thinly sliced
8 slices Beefsteak tomato (1/4-inch-thick)
8 slices Whole-grain bread (about 1/4 inch thick)
2 slices Italian style loaf bread
1 Garlic clove, halved
1 1/3 cups packaged Baby Arugula and spinach greens
2 teaspoons Country-style Dijon mustard
1 teaspoon Olive oil
1 teaspoon Powdered Sugar for cooking spray

METHOD:

1. Give your sandwich a rich garlic flavor by brushing one side of each bread slice with oil and rubbing cut sides of garlic over oiled side.
2. Spread 1/2 teaspoon Dijon mustard on 4 bread slices with oil side down.

3. Place 1 ounce cheese, 1/3 cup greens, and 2 tomato slices on each bread slice on which you put the mustard.

4. Now place the remaining 4 bread slices on the top with oil side up.

5. Set your grill to high heat.

6. Coat each sandwich with cooking spray and place 2 at a time on the grill rack.

7. Grill for 2 minutes on each side or until the bread is lightly toasted and the cheese melts.

5. Cream Cheese Grilled Sandwiches with Biscoff and banana

Preparation Time: 5 minutes
Cooking Time: 8 – 10 minutes
Ready In: 15 minutes
Servings: makes 1 sandwich

INGREDIENTS:

1 medium sized Banana, sliced
2 tablespoons Creamy Biscoff spread
2 ounces Cream Cheese, thinly sliced
2 teaspoons Honey
2 slices Sandwich bread
Butter as required for cooking

METHOD:

1. Start with the yummy step of cooking the banana slices in drops of honey for 3-4 minutes on each side until they are caramelized and turn golden brown. Remove from the pan and keep aside.
2. Make your bread slices crispy by applying butter to one side and heating them on medium heat in a flat pan, butter side down.
3. Apply 1 tablespoon of Biscoff spread on the bread and top it with the caramelized bananas and cream cheese.

4. Apply the remaining Biscoff spread on the other slice of bread and place it on top of the cream cheese, butter side up.

5. Cook the sandwich for 3-4 minutes on each side in the flat pan until the bread is toasted and the cream cheese is melted. Serve warm!

6. Provolone Cheese Grilled Sandwiches with Fried Egg

Preparation Time: 5 – 7 minutes
Cooking Time: 10 – 12 minutes
Ready In: 20 minutes
Servings: makes 2 sandwiches

INGREDIENTS:

8 thin slices Provolone Cheese
4 Large Eggs
12 slices Pancetta (Italian bacon)
4 slices Sourdough bread
12 Fresh Basil leaves
1 small Green onion, chopped
2 tablespoons Butter
Parmesan cheese shavings as required

METHOD:

1. Heat a large nonstick pan or skillet to medium heat and put in a generous amount of butter. Cook the pancetta bacon in it until crisp.
2. Again melt some butter in the skillet over medium heat and add 4 bread slices.
3. On top of each bread slice, place 2 provolone cheese slices and sprinkle them with black pepper.

4. Keep the bread on the pan until the cheese melts. This should take approximately 3 to 4 minutes. This will result in 4 beautiful cheese toasts.

5. Side-by-side in another large pan, crack the eggs and cook them until the whites are set but yolks are still runny. This should take 2 to 3 minutes.

6. After the cheese toasts have cooled down a little place 3 pancetta slices and 2 eggs on top of each of 2 cheese toasts.

7. Top the eggs with onion, Parmesan cheese shavings and basil and then cover them with the remaining bread slices, cheese side down.

8. Cut the sandwiches in half and serve warm.

7. Mozzarella Cheese Grilled Sandwiches with Veggies

Preparation Time: 12-15 minutes
Cooking Time: 20 minutes
Ready In: 35 minutes
Servings: makes 4 sandwiches

INGREDIENTS:

5 ounces Fresh Mozzarella cheese, sliced
1 Red or yellow bell pepper, seeded and cut into 4 pieces
3 cups Zucchini, diagonally cut (1/8-inch-thick)
2 tablespoons Balsamic Vinegar
1 teaspoon Extravirgin Olive oil
3 Red onion slices (1/8-inch-thick)
¼ teaspoon freshly ground Black Pepper
Salt as per taste
8 Fresh Basil leaves
1 cup Gourmet salad greens
1 Ciabatta/ Focaccia bread loaf (1-pound), cut in half horizontally
Cooking spray   as required

METHOD:

1. Take a large bowl. Combine the zucchini, bell pepper and red onions and dress them nicely with vinegar,

olive oil, salt and black pepper. Take out the extra dressing and remove the vegetables from the bowl.

2. Place the zucchini on a medium pre-heated grill rack coated with cooking spray and grill for around 3 minutes on each side or until it becomes tender.

3. Then grill the peppers and onion slices for about 7 minutes on each side or until they become tender.

4. Remove the center core of the bread loaf leaving a ½ inch thick outer shell.

5. Fill the grilled vegetables, greens, cheese and basil in the emptied bread shell and pour the remaining dressing on it.

6. Cover the shell with the top of the bread and press lightly.

7. Put this filled sandwich on the grill rack and grill for about 4 minutes or until the cheese melts. Cut into quarters and serve hot!

8. White Cheddar Cheese Grilled Sandwiches with Avocado & Tomatoes

Preparation Time: 8 minutes
Cooking Time: 12 minutes
Ready In: 20 minutes
Servings: makes 2 sandwiches

INGREDIENTS:

4 ounces Sharp White Cheddar cheese slices
1 Avocado
8-10 Grape/Baby Tomatoes, sliced in half
4 Whole Wheat Bread slices
1 teaspoon Lemon juice
As per taste Salt
Butter as required for cooking

METHOD:

1. Prepare the avocado first by removing its pit and scooping the core out into a small bowl. Mash the scooped avocado with lemon juice and salt and keep aside.
2. Apply butter smoothly on the outside of one slice of bread and lay a quarter of the white cheddar cheese on the unbuttered side of the bread.

3. Top that with about half the prepared avocado paste and several tomato halves.

4. Place another quarter of the cheese on top of that and then cover it with the other slice of bread.

5. Butter the outside of the top slice of bread.

6. Place this sandwich in a frying pan over medium heat. When the bottom piece of bread turns to a slight brown color, flip the sandwich and do the same to the other side.

7. Cook until the cheese is melted and repeat with the other sandwich.

9. Fontina Cheese Grilled Sandwiches with Honey & Basil

Preparation Time: 5 – 7 minutes
Cooking Time: 10 - 12 minutes
Ready In: 18 – 20 minutes
Servings: makes 2 sandwiches

INGREDIENTS:

10 slices Fontina cheese,
3 oz. Mozzarella cheese
12 to 16 Large Basil leaves
6 Strawberry Tomatoes,
4 slices bread
Honey
Butter

METHOD:

1. Apply butter smoothly on one side of each slice of bread.
2. On the other side of any 2 slices, spread as much honey as you prefer but it should be enough to cover the bread's surface.
3. Place tomato slices on the honey coated surface of the bread slices.
4. Top the tomatoes with 4 slices each of Fontina cheese.

5. Cover the Fontina cheese with fresh basil leaves topped by sliced mozzarella. Now cover the sandwich with the remaining slice of bread with the buttered side up.

6. Take a medium sized flat pan and keep it on low heat. Place one sandwich on the pan and let each side grill for 3 to 5 minutes or until it turns slightly brown.

7. Repeat with the other sandwich. Serve hot!

10. Goat Cheese Grilled Sandwiches with Bell Peppers & Portobello

Preparation Time: 5 – 7 minutes
Cooking Time: 10 - 12 minutes
Ready In: 18 – 20 minutes
Servings: makes 2 sandwiches

INGREDIENTS:

½ cup Goat cheese
1 Red bell pepper, cut in half and seeded
1 Yellow bell pepper, cut in half and seeded
4 Portobello Mushroom caps
1/3 cup Fresh Basil, chopped
4 Kaiser rolls
¼ teaspoon freshly ground black pepper
Salt as per taste
¼ cup Balsamic vinegar
1 tablespoon Olive oil
1 Garlic clove, minced
Butter
Cooking spray   as required

METHOD:

1. Prepare a dressing in a bowl with vinegar, olive oil and garlic cloves.

2. Add the colorful bell peppers and mushrooms to this dressing and coat them nicely. When done, remove the veggies from the dressing and keep aside.

3. Coat the grill rack lightly with cooking spray and keep the dressed vegetables on it on medium-high heat. Let them cook for about 4 minutes on each side or until they are tender.

4. When done, remove the veggies from the grill and let them cool down slightly. After that, cut the bell peppers into thin strips.

5. Mix basil, salt and black pepper in a bowl and add the bell pepper strips to this. Mix nicely.

6. Cut the Kaiser rolls in half horizontally. These will become our sandwiches. Spread the soft goat cheese smoothly over the cut side of the rolls.

7. Place one mushroom cap on the bottom half of each sliced roll and top that with around $1/3^{rd}$ cup of the pepper strips mixture. Cover with the other half of the roll.

8. Prepare your grill rack by coating slightly with cooking spray and place the sandwiches on it. Press them lightly with a heavy iron object.

9. Grill for 3 minutes or until the bread is toasted.

11. Provolone Cheese Grilled Sandwiches with Sloppy Joes

Preparation Time: 10 minutes
Cooking Time: 10 minutes
Ready In: 20 – 25 minutes
Servings: makes 1 sandwich

INGREDIENTS:

2 slices Sandwich bread
2 slices Provolone cheese
2 tablespoons Butter
1/3 cup Sloppy Joe mixture

INGREDIENTS FOR SLOPPY JOE MIXTURE:

½ cup Yellow pepper, chopped
1 pound Lean Ground Beef
1 cup Onion, chopped
1 tablespoon Brown sugar
2 tablespoons Spicy mustard
8 Dinner rolls, cut in half
1 cup Low-sugar organic ketchup
1 tablespoon Vinegar
1/8 teaspoon Cloves
2 tablespoons Olive oil
Salt and Pepper as required

METHOD FOR PREPARING SLOPPY JOW MIXTURE:

1. Sauté the onions in olive oil in a large pan over medium-high heat until they are fragrant. This should take about 2 minutes.
2. Add in the peppers and cook them until they are soft.
3. To this, add the ground beef and cook until it is fully browned. This should take about 6 - 7 minutes.
4. Drain the beef mixture and return it to the stove.
5. To this, add brown sugar, vinegar, ketchup, mustard and salt and pepper and stir nicely. Mixture is ready.

METHOD FOR PREPARING SLOPPY JOE GRILLED SANDWICH:

1. Apply liberal quantity of butter to one side of each slice of bread. Use about one tablespoon butter for each side.
2. Place a slice of cheese on each unbuttered side and top this with sloppy Joe mixture. Cover with the other slice.
3. Heat a pan over medium heat and cook the sandwich until the cheese is melted and the bread is crispy and brown.

12. Cheddar Cheese Grilled Sandwiches with Green Apple

Preparation Time: 5 minutes
Cooking Time: 6 minutes
Ready In: 10 – 12 minutes
Servings: makes 1 sandwich

INGREDIENTS:

2 Thinly sliced slices Walnut/Flax Bread
1 ounce Vermont extra-sharp aged cheddar cheese, thinly sliced
3 – 4 thin slices Crisp Tart Apple, such as Granny Smith
1 tablespoon Unsalted butter, softened

METHOD:

1. Apply butter evenly on one side of each slice of bread.
2. On one side of bread place half of the cheese, sufficient apple slices, and the remaining cheese. Then, close the sandwich with the second slice of bread, buttered side up.
3. Heat a large pan on low-medium heat and grill the sandwich until the bread is toasted and the cheese is melted. This should take around 3 minutes per side.

13. Mozzarella Cheese Grilled Sandwiches with Zucchini

Preparation Time: 10 minutes
Cooking Time: 5 minutes
Ready In: 15 minutes
Servings: makes 4 sandwiches

INGREDIENTS:

1 medium Zucchini, trimmed and cut lengthwise into 6 slices
6 ounces Fresh Mozzarella cheese, thinly sliced
4 Ciabatta rolls, split and toasted
8 large Fresh Basil leaves
1 medium Tomato, thinly sliced
1½ teaspoons Balsamic Vinegar
4 Extra-virgin olive oil   teaspoons, divided
1/8 teaspoon kosher salt
1 Garlic clove, minced
1/8 teaspoon Black pepper

METHOD:

1. Toss the zucchini with the olive oil and garlic such that it is coated.
2. Add it in a heated grill pan over medium-high heat. Cook for about 2 minutes.

3. Remove the zucchini from the pan and put it in a shallow dish. Pour vinegar drops on it and sprinkle salt and pepper. Mix nicely.
4. Apply olive oil on the bottom halves of the split ciabatta rolls.
5. Spread the zucchini, basil tomatoes and mozzarella cheese on the oiled sides.
6. Apply the remaining liquid from the shallow dish on the top halves of the split ciabatta rolls and cover the sandwiches with them.
7. Heat the sandwiches in the pan over low heat until they are warm or cheese starts to melt.

14. 4 Cheese White pizza Grilled Sandwiches

Preparation Time: 7 – 8 minutes
Cooking Time: 6 – 7 minutes
Ready In: 15 minutes
Servings: makes 4 sandwiches

INGREDIENTS:

4 ounces Mozzarella cheese, finely shredded
2 tablespoons Parmesan cheese, grated
¼ cup Ricotta cheese
2 thin slices Provolone cheese
4-6 slices Fresh ciabatta bread
1 tablespoon Olive oil
¾ teaspoon Italian seasoning
Kosher salt as per taste
1 Garlic clove, minced
1/8 teaspoon Black pepper

METHOD:

1. Mix the different varieties of cheese with olive oil, minced garlic, Italian seasoning, salt and pepper.
2. Lightly oil one side of each slice of bread.
3. Add equal amount of the prepared mixture to the un-oiled side of two slices of bread.

4. Cover with the other slice of bread with the oiled side out and place the sandwich on a skillet that has been heated over medium heat.

5. Cook till one side is toasted, carefully flip and toast other side. Serve hot.

15. Mozzarella, Cheddar & Cream Cheese Grilled Panini with Green Goddess salad

Preparation Time: 15 minutes
Cooking Time: 15 minutes
Ready In: 30 minutes
Servings: makes 4 panini

INGREDIENTS:

1 cup Mozzarella cheese, shredded
1 cup Sharp Cheddar, shredded
2 ounces Cream cheese, cut into small cubes
8-12 slices Sourdough bread
1 Oil-packed Anchovy, finely chopped
2 tablespoons Fresh Tarragon, chopped
3 tablespoons Fresh Italian parsley, chopped
2 tablespoons Fresh Cilantro, chopped
1 tablespoon Fresh Basil, chopped
1 teaspoon Lime zest, (about 1 lime)
1 tablespoon Shallot, finely chopped
1 Garlic clove, finely chopped
¼ teaspoon Dijon mustard
2 tablespoons Extra-virgin olive oil

METHOD:

1. Fine-chop the anchovies and garlic clove so that they become almost like a paste.
2. To this, add all the herbs, lime zest, mustard and cream cheese and grind in a food processor until they are well blended.
3. Take this mixture out in a bowl of medium size and add in the mozzarella and cheddar cheese.
4. Apply a sufficient amount of this mixture on one side of each slice of bread and close the sandwich with the other slice.
5. Brush the top of the sandwich with a little olive oil and grill the Panini on medium-high heat for 5 to 6 minutes or until the bread is toasted and the cheese melts.

16. Provolone Cheese Grilled Sandwiches with Roast Beef and Caramelized Onion

Preparation Time: 5 minutes
Cooking Time: 20 minutes
Ready In: 25 minutes
Servings: makes 1 sandwich

INGREDIENTS:

¼ pound Roast beef slices
2 slices Hearty bread
1 Red onion, sliced into ¼ inch rings
2 tablespoons Butter, divided
5 slices Provolone or American cheese

METHOD:

1. Caramelize the onions in a pan with about 1 tablespoon of butter over medium heat until the onions become soft and fragrant. This should take about 10 – 15 minutes.
2. Warm the roast beef slices on low heat to make them ready.
3. Apply butter generously on both slices of the hearty bread.

4. In a pre-heated pan, place the buttered slice of bread with the buttered side down.

5. In the pan itself, add 2 slices of cheese, warm roast beef and caramelized onions and the remaining cheese slices on the bread.

6. Cover with the other slice of bread with the buttered side up.

7. Grill on the pan by pressing lightly until the bread is toasted to a nice brown color. This should take about 4 – 5 minutes. Serve hot!

17. Fontina Cheese Grilled Panini with Prosciutto Ham & Figs

Preparation Time: 5 minutes
Cooking Time: 4 - 5 minutes
Ready In: 10 minutes
Servings: makes 4 sandwiches

INGREDIENTS:

1¼ cups Fontina cheese, shredded
4 ounces Prosciutto Ham, very thinly sliced
8 slices crusty Chicago-style Italian bread
½ cup Baby arugula leaves
¼ cup Fig preserves
Olive oil-flavored cooking spray as required

METHOD:

1. Spread the Fontina cheese, prosciutto and arugula evenly on each of the 4 bread slices.
2. Top each of these with 1 teaspoon of fig preserves. Cover the sandwiches with the remaining bread slices.
3. Heat Panini grill to medium-low and place the cooking spray coated sandwiches on it.
4. Let them grill for about 3 to 4 minutes or until the bread is golden brown and the cheese starts to melt.
5. If you prefer, cut the Panini in half before serving.

18. Gruyere Surchoix Cheese Grilled Sandwiches with Toasted Almonds

Preparation Time: 5 minutes
Cooking Time: 20 minutes
Ready In: 25 minutes
Servings: makes 4 sandwiches

INGREDIENTS:

4 slices Cinnamon Bread
½ cup Toasted Almonds
1 cup Gruyere Surchoix, finely grated
½ teaspoon Powdered Sugar
Unsalted butter as required for cooking

METHOD:

1. Lightly butter one side of each of the cinnamon bread slices.
2. Spread the grated cheese on the non-buttered side of 2 of the slices.
2. Top the cheese with toasted almonds generously and sprinkle a little powdered sugar over it. Cover the sandwiches with the other 2 slices of bread, buttered side up.
3. Heat a pan over medium-low heat and place the sandwich one at a time on the pan, buttered side down.

4. Press gently while cooking and leave it on till the bread is a nice golden brown or cheese starts to melt.
5. Serve warm!

19. Gruyere Cheese Grilled Sandwiches with Olives & Tomatoes

Preparation Time: 10 – 12 minutes
Cooking Time: 7 – 8 minutes
Ready In: 20 minutes
Servings: makes 4 sandwiches

INGREDIENTS:

2 ounces Gruyere cheese, shaved
¼ cup Parmigiano-Reggiano cheese, grated
1 (8.5-ounce) jar Oil-packed sun-dried Tomatoes
8 slices Multigrain bread
8 Large Tomato slices   (1/4-inch-thick)
12 Kalamata olives, pitted
2 Garlic cloves

METHOD:

1. Grind 4 sun-dried tomatoes, olives and garlic in 1 tablespoon oil from the oil-packed jar of tomatoes until they become a smooth paste.
2. Take another 1 tablespoon of oil from the jar and brush one side of each of the bread slices with it.
3. On the non-oiled side of 4 slices apply about 1 ½ tablespoons of the paste we made in step 1.
4. On top of that, spread 1 tablespoon Parmigiano-Reggiano cheese and then top that with 2 tomato slices

and Gruyere cheese. Cover the sandwiches with the remaining 4 slices with the oiled side up.

5. In a medium-high heated pan, add 2 sandwiches at a time. Place a heavy object iron object on top of the sandwiches so that they are pressed lightly.

6. Cook for about 2 minutes on each side or until the bread is toasted and cheese melts.

7. Repeat with the other 2 sandwiches. Serve hot!

20. Colby Jack Cheese Grilled Sandwiches with Nachos

Preparation Time: 5 minutes
Cooking Time: 12 – 15 minutes
Ready In: 20 minutes
Servings: makes 4 sandwiches

INGREDIENTS:

8 pieces Colby Jack cheese
1 Jar Nacho cheese or Pimento cheese sauce
1 Bag Tortilla chips
Small can Black olives (sliced or chopped)
Pickled/Fresh jalapeños (if pickled – Small jar, if fresh – 1, seeded and cut into slices)
4 English muffins
2 tablespoons Green onion, chopped
1 can Black beans, drained and rinsed
1 Jar Salsa or homemade pico de gallo
1 small container Sour cream
Prepared guacamole as required
Butter   as required

METHOD:

1. Cut the English muffins into halves from the middle (top and bottom should be separated).

2. Keep a large frying pan over medium-high heat and place 4 bottom pieces of the muffins in melted butter in the pan. The inside of the bottom half should be down. Cook for about 2 – 4 minutes till the bottoms become crisp.
3. Remove the bottoms from the pan and repeat step 2 with the muffin tops.
4. Apply one slice of Colby Jack cheese, plenty of tortilla chips, sufficient amount of black beans, a few jalapeño slices, spoonfuls of chopped green onion, sliced olives, salsa or pica de gallo, and nacho cheese or pimento sauce on each English muffin cut bottom. Top all of this with another slice Colby Jack cheese.
5. Heat your oven to 350 degrees F and place the sandwiches without the tops in a low baking dish in the oven. Bake the sandwiches for about 6 – 8 minutes or until the cheese is completely melted.
6. After removing from the oven, put a scoop of sour cream, guacamole and additional salsa and other ingredients as your prefer and cover the sandwiches with the muffin tops.
7. Serve hot!

21. Macaroni & Cheese Grilled Sandwiches with Pulled Pork & Barbecue Sauce

Preparation Time: 10 minutes
Cooking Time: 30 minutes
Ready In: 40 minutes
Servings: makes 4 sandwiches

INGREDIENTS:

4 cups Prepared Macaroni and Cheese, warmed
2 Onions, thinly sliced
2 cups Prepared Pulled Pork
8 slices Sourdough Bread
1 cup Barbecue Sauce
12 slices Sharp Cheddar Cheese
4 tablespoons Unsalted Butter, divided
Kosher salt and freshly ground pepper as required

METHOD:

1. Start with solidifying your macaroni & cheese. Spread the mac and cheese in a medium sized baking dish and cover it with plastic wrap. Keep it in the fridge for about 45 minutes so that it becomes firm.

2. While that is being done, caramelize the onions in butter seasoned with salt and pepper. This should take about 15 minutes.

3. Heat the pulled pork in a sauce pan with the barbeque sauce over low heat for about 5 minutes.

4. Remove the mac and cheese from the fridge. They should have become firm. Cut them into squares slightly smaller in size than your bread slices.

5. Brush one side of each bread slice with butter and on the other side, place 1 slice of cheddar cheese, 1 mac & cheese square, another slice of cheddar, pulled pork, caramelized onions and another slice of cheddar – in that order.

6. Cover the sandwiches with the remaining slices of bread with the buttered side up.

7. Cook the sandwich over medium heat in a pan until the cheese melts or the bread turns slightly brown.

22. Muenster Cheese Grilled Sandwiches with Ham & Spinach

Preparation Time: 5 minutes
Cooking Time: 5 – 6 minutes
Ready In: 10 – 12 minutes
Servings: makes 4 sandwiches

INGREDIENTS:

2 cups Fresh Baby Spinach
4 slices Muenster cheese
8 ounces Deli Ham, thinly sliced
8 slices crusty Chicago-style Italian bread, toasted
¼ cup Mild chowchow
Cooking spray   as required

METHOD:

1. On 4 slices of bread place 1 slice Muenster cheese, 2 ounces ham, ½ cup baby spinach and 1 tablespoon chowchow. Cover with the other slice of bread.
2. Coat the sandwiches with cooking spray and place on a pan over medium-high heat.
3. Cook for 2 – 3 minutes on each side or until the bread turns slightly brown or cheese starts to melt.

23. Parmesan & Mozzarella Cheese Grilled Sandwiches with Spinach Artichoke dip

Preparation Time: 5 minutes
Cooking Time: 35 minutes
Ready In: 40 minutes
Servings: makes 4 sandwiches

INGREDIENTS:

1 cup Mozzarella cheese, shredded
1 cup Parmesan cheese, grated
8 slices Pumpernickel Bread
½ cup Mayonnaise (low-fat mayonnaise or sour cream can be substituted)
14 ounce jar Artichoke hearts, drained, chopped, marinated and quartered
10 ounce package Frozen, Chopped Spinach, thawed and pressed of its liquid
8 ounce package Cream cheese, room temperature (low-fat can be used)
½ teaspoon Garlic powder
2-3 tablespoons Butter

METHOD:

1. Mix all types of cheese together with mayonnaise, spinach, artichokes and garlic powder in a bowl and bake this mixture for 20 – 25 minutes at 350 degrees F.
2. Apply butter smoothly on one side of each of the bread slices and spread the baked mixture on the other side of 4 of the slices. Cover with the remaining 4 slices.
3. In a pan, place the sandwich with the buttered side down and cook for about 2 minutes on each side. Be careful while flipping. Serve hot!

24. Cheddar Cheese Grilled Sandwiches with Piquillo peppers

Preparation Time: 5 – 7 minutes
Cooking Time: 4 minutes
Ready In: 11 – 12 minutes
Servings: makes 1 sandwich

INGREDIENTS:

12 oz. Extra Sharp cheddar cheese
5-6 oz. Red bell or Piquillo peppers, roasted
½ cup Best Foods mayonnaise
2 slices Sourdough bread
4 Garlic Cloves
Butter   as required
Salt and pepper as per taste

METHOD:

1. Grind the cheese until it becomes fine like gravel.
2. To this, add garlic and the peppers and grind again till the mixture blends finely.
3. Add mayonnaise, salt and pepper to this and mix again.
4. Butter one side of both bread slices and on the other side of 1 slice, apply the mixture smoothly. Cover with the second slice.

5. Cook the sandwich in a pan over medium heat until the bread becomes light brown or the cheese melts.

25. Manchego Cheese Grilled Panini with Mushrooms & Shallots

Preparation Time: 2 – 3 minutes
Cooking Time: 17 – 18 minutes
Ready In: 20 minutes
Servings: makes 4 sandwiches

INGREDIENTS:

2 packages Pre-sliced exotic mushroom blend
1 package Pre-sliced cremini mushrooms
1 tablespoon Fresh Thyme, chopped
8 slices Sourdough bread
3 ounces Manchego cheese, shaved
¼ cup minced Shallots
2 teaspoons minced Fresh Garlic
1½ tablespoons Sherry Vinegar
Butter   as required
¼ teaspoon Kosher Salt
½ teaspoon freshly ground Black Pepper
1 teaspoon Unsalted Butter
Cooking spray   as required

METHOD:

1. Cook shallots, thyme, mushroom blend, cremini mushrooms and fresh garlic for 10 minutes in butter in a large pan over medium-high heat and season them

with salt and pepper. Continue to cook until the liquid from the mushrooms almost evaporates and the mushrooms become tender. Stir frequently.

2. To this, add vinegar and cook for only about 30 seconds – just enough for the liquid to evaporate.

3. Apply the mushroom mixture on 4 slices of bread and spread Manchego cheese over that evenly. Cover the sandwiches with the remaining slices of bread.

4. Coat a large pan with cooking spray and place 2 sandwiches in it over medium-high heat. Place a heavy iron object on the sandwiches and press gently to flatten.

5. Cook the sandwiches for about 2 minutes on each side or until the cheese melts and the bread turns slightly brown. Repeat with other 2 sandwiches.

26. Brie Cheese Grilled Sandwiches with Raspberries & Nutella

Preparation Time: 5 minutes
Cooking Time: 5 minutes
Ready In: 10 minutes
Servings: makes 1 sandwich

INGREDIENTS:

3 slices Brie cheese
6 fresh Raspberries
2 slices Crusty bread
2 tablespoons Nutella
2 tablespoons Unsalted Butter

METHOD:

1. Apply butter on one side of each slice of bread. On the unbuttered side spread Nutella generously.
2. Top this with the brie cheese and raspberries. Cover the sandwich with the other slice, buttered side up.
3. Place the sandwich in a pan over medium heat and cook till the bread is toasted or the cheese starts to melt. Repeat for the other side. Serve immediately.

27. American Cheese Grilled Sandwiches with Cheese Sticks

Preparation Time: 5 minutes
Cooking Time: 5 minutes
Ready In: 10 minutes
Servings: makes 1 sandwich

INGREDIENTS:

2 slices Sourdough bread
4 slices American cheese
3 prepared Cheese sticks
2 teaspoons Softened butter

METHOD:

1. Apply butter on one side of each slice of bread. On the unbuttered side spread American cheese generously. You might want to break the slice into small pieces for this.
2. Top this with the prepared cheese sticks placed at equal distances from each other.
3. On top of the cheese sticks spread the remaining American cheese and cover with the other slice of bread, buttered side up.
4. Place the sandwich in a pan over medium heat and cook till the bread is toasted. Repeat for the other side.

28. Cheddar Cheese Grilled Sandwiches with Beef & Onions

Preparation Time: 20 – 22 minutes
Cooking Time: 10 – 12 minutes
Ready In: 35 minutes
Servings: makes 4 sandwiches

INGREDIENTS:

8 slices Sourdough bread
4 slices Reduced-fat processed Sharp Cheddar Cheese
2 cups Onion, coarsely chopped
1 pound Ground round (beef)
2 teaspoons Butter, divided
1/8 teaspoon Salt
¼ teaspoon Freshly ground black pepper
Cooking spray   as required

METHOD:

1. Sauté the onions in 1 teaspoon butter over medium-high heat until golden brown. This should take about 3 – 4 minutes. Then reduce the heat and continue to cook the onions until they become tender. This should take about 10 minutes.
2. Marinate the beef with salt and pepper in a bowl. Make 4 oval-shaped patties out of this beef mixture.

3. Place these patties on a broiler pan coated with cooking spray and broil for 3 – 4 minutes on each side until done.

4. On 4 bread slices, place one cheese slice, one beef patty and 3 tablespoons of onion mixture each. Cover the sandwich with the remaining bread slices.

5. Apply butter smoothly on the outer slices of the sandwiches and place 2 sandwiches at a time on a cooking spray coated pan over medium heat.

6. Cook for 3 – 4 minutes on each side or until bread turns slightly brown and cheese starts to melt.

7. Serve hot!

29. Cheddar Cheese Grilled Sandwiches with Ham & Pineapple

Preparation Time: 5 minutes
Cooking Time: 10 minutes
Ready In: 15 minutes
Servings: makes 4 sandwiches

INGREDIENTS:

8 thin slices Smoked deli Ham
8 thin slices Sharp Cheddar Cheese
4 Pineapple rings
4 Ciabatta rolls
4 tablespoons unsalted butter

METHOD:

1. Cut the Ciabatta rolls into halves from the center so that they separate into a top and a bottom half.
2. Place 1 slice of cheese, 2 slices of ham, 1 pineapple ring and then another cheese slice on each of the Ciabatta bottom half. Cover with the top half.
3. Apply butter smoothly on the outer surface of the top and bottom half of the sandwiches.
4. Cook the sandwiches on a pan over medium-low heat till the roll is toasted and becomes light brown. Serve hot!

30. Havarti & Cheddar Cheese Grilled Sandwiches with Garlic & Green Onion Mashed Potato

Preparation Time: 10 – 15 minutes
Cooking Time: 5 – 6 minutes
Ready In: 20 minutes
Servings: makes 2 sandwiches

INGREDIENTS:

½ cup Green Onion, chopped
1 cup Wisconsin Dofino Creamy Havarti Cheese, finely grated
4 slices Great Lakes Sharp Cheddar
4 slices Italian/Country Bread
½ cup Homemade Garlic Green Onion Mashed Potatoes
½ cup Broccoli, steamed
2 tablespoons unsalted butter
Salt and pepper as per taste

METHOD FOR MAKING GARLIC & GREEN ONION MASHED POTATOES:

1. Boil and mash 2 - 3 medium sized potatoes.
2. Add finely chopped garlic and green onions.
3. Add salt and pepper to taste.

4. To this, add about 2 tablespoons of milk and 2 teaspoons of room temperature butter.
5. Mix all of these nicely to form a creamy mixture.
6. You can even add a little of the Havarti and cheddar cheese to this to give it more flavor.

METHOD FOR PREPARING THE SANDWICH:

1. Sauté the steamed broccoli with green onions, a little butter, salt and pepper till it is tender yet still crunchy.
2. Apply butter to one side of each slice of bread. On the unbuttered side of 2 slices place 1 slice of the cheddar cheese, about 2 tablespoons of the mashed potatoes, the sautéed broccoli and finally top that with the grated havarti cheese. Cover with the remaining slices of bread.
3. Place the sandwiches in a pan over medium-high heat and cook the sandwiches for about 3 minutes on each side or until the bread is toasted and the cheese has started to melt. Serve hot!

31. Cream Cheese Grilled Bagel Sandwiches

Preparation Time: 5 – 7 minutes
Cooking Time: 4 – 5 minutes
Ready In: 10 – 12 minutes
Servings: makes 1 sandwich

INGREDIENTS:

1 handful Baby Hierloom Tomatoes, sliced in half
1 Common Bagel
1 teaspoon Fresh Thyme
2 heaping tablespoons Organic Cream Cheese
1 teaspoon Salted Butter

METHOD:

1. Cut the bagel in half and place it flat side down. Scoop out the top and bottom of the bagel with a spoon.
2. Apply cream cheese generously on the scooped bagel halves.
3. On the bottom half of the bagel, arrange tomato slices on top of the cream cheese.
4. Evenly sprinkle 1 teaspoon of the thyme leaves on the other half of the bagel. Place this half over the tomato covered half.

5. Apply butter evenly on the top and bottom surfaces of the bagel and place the sandwich in a pan over medium heat. Cook for about 3 minutes on each side or until the sides start to turn brown, serve hot!

Part 2

Dialysis Cookbook DIALYSIS DIET COOKBOOK

BREAKFAST

1. Maple Sausage

Yield: 12 Serving

Ingredients

1 pound ground pork or beef

1/2 pound ground turkey

1/2 teaspoon black pepper

3/4 teaspoon dried sage (or 2 tablespoons fresh)

1/4 teaspoon mace or nutmeg

1/4 teaspoon ground all spice

2 teaspoons maple syrup

1 teaspoon water

Directions

1. Mix all ingredients in a large bowl.

2. Refrigerate for at least 4 hours, or overnight.

Form into patties and cook in skillet over medium-high heat until well browned, or about 10 minutes.

Lemon-Blueberry Corn Muffins Yield: 12 Serving

Ingredients

3/4 cup yellow cornmeal

3/4 cup whole wheat flour

1 1/2 teaspoons baking powder

1/4 cup granulated sugar

3/4 cup milk (cow's, soy, or rice)

2 tablespoons oil or unsalted butter, melted

1 egg, beaten

2 tablespoons lemon juice

1 teaspoon lemon zest

1 cup frozen or fresh blueberries Directions

1. Preheat oven to 400 degrees.

2. Spray muffin pan or 8×8 baking pan with non-stick cooking spray.

3. Combine cornmeal, flour, baking powder and sugar in a large mixing bowl.

Combine milk, oil or butter, egg, lemon juice

and lemon zest in a small bowl.

5. Add milk mixture to cornmeal mixture and stir until just barely mixed. It is ok to have some

lumps.

6. Then lightly stir in blueberries (if you are using frozen berries rinse them with cold water and pat dry before adding to the batter).

7. Pour batter into muffin or 8×8 pan.

8. Bake for 15 minutes if making muffins, 25

minutes if baking in 8×8 pan.

9. Drizzle with honey if desired.

Lemon Apple Honey Smoothie

Yield: 4 (2/3 Cup) Serving

Ingredients

1/4 cup lemon juice

1/2 cup apple juice

1 apple, peeled and cored

1 banana

2-3 teaspoons honey

1 cup vanilla yogurt, frozen Directions

1. Combine all ingredients in a blender and mix until smooth.

2. Pour into a tall chilled glass.

Puffy Chili Rellenos Casserole

Yield: 8 Serving

Ingredients

6 ounces cheddar cheese, shredded

6 ounces jack cheese, shredded

1 cup ricotta cheese

8 fresh padillia peppers, whole

8 large eggs

2/3 cup milk

1 cup flour

1 teaspoon baking powder, low sodium Directions

1. Preheat oven to 350 degrees.

2. Roast peppers and remove skins. See roasting instructions below.

3. Put cheese and ricotta in peppers and arrange

in a greased 9×13 pan.

4. In blender or food processor beat eggs, milk, flour, and baking powder until smooth.

5. Pour evenly over peppers.

Bake for 30-40 minutes.

7. Serve hot.

To Roast peppers: Turn broiler to 500 degrees. Broil, watching carefully, until slightly charred. Remove

from oven, put in bowl and cover with plastic wrap.

Let sit for about 15 minutes then peel off the thin clear skin of the peppers.

Mexican Brunch Eggs

Yield: 8 Serving

Ingredients

1/2 cup chopped onion

2 cloves garlic, crushed

2 tablespoons margarine

1 1/2 cups frozen corn, thawed

1 1/2 teaspoons ground cumin

1/8 teaspoon cayenne pepper

8 eggs, beaten

8 slices toasted bread

Directions

1. In a large skillet, saute onion and garlic in margarine until onion is soft.

2. Add corn, cumin, and cayenne; stir to combine.

3. Pour in eggs or egg substitute and cook over low heat, stirring occasionally until eggs are set.

4. Arrange toast triangles on a large platter.

5. Spoon egg mixture on toast triangles.

6. Serve immediately.

Master Mix

Yield: 13 Servings

Ingredients

8 1/2 cups all-purpose flour

1 tablespoon baking powder

2 teaspoons cream of tartar

1 teaspoon baking soda

1 1/2 cups instant nonfat milk powder

2 1/4 cups vegetable shortening Directions

1. Sift together flour, baking powder, cream of tartar, baking soda, and milk powder.

2. Cut in shortening with a pastry blender until evenly distributed.

3. Store in a large, airtight container in a cool, dry place.

4. Use within 10-12 weeks.

40-Second Omelet

Yield: 1 Serving

Ingredients

2 eggs

2 tablespoons water

1 tablespoon unsalted butter

1/2 cup filling (vegetables, meat, seafood) Directions

1. Beat together eggs and water until blended.

2. In a 10-inch omelet pan or fry pan, heat butter until just hot enough to sizzle a drop of water.

3. Pour in egg mixture. Mixture should set at edges right away. With an inverted pancake turner, carefully push cooked portions at edges toward center so uncooked portions can reach the hot pan surface. Tilt pan and move as necessary.

4. Continue until egg is set and will not flow. Fill the omelet with 1/2 cup of vegetables, meat, or seafood filling, if desired. Put filling on left side

Dialysis Cookbook if you're right handed and the right side if you're

left handed.

5. With the pancake turner, fold omelet in half.

Invert onto a plate with the omelet's bottom side facing up.

Apple Bran Muffins

Yield: 12 Servings

Ingredients

2 cups whole wheat flour

1 1/2 cups wheat bran

1 1/4 teaspoons baking soda

1/2 teaspoon nutmeg

1 tablespoon orange rind (grated)

1 cup chopped apple

1/2 cup raisins

1/2 cup chopped nuts or sunflower seeds

juice from 1 orange

scant 2 cups buttermilk or sour milk

1 beaten egg

1/2 cup molasses

2 tablespoons oil

Directions

1. Preheat oven to 350 degrees.

2. Toss flour, bran, baking soda, and nutmeg together with fork.

Stir in orange rind, apples, raisins, and nuts or seeds.

4. Pour the juice of 1 orange into a 2 cup measure and add buttermilk to make 2 cups.

5. Combine buttermilk mixture with egg, molasses, and oil; stir thoroughly.

6. Stir liquid ingredients into dry ingredients with a few swift strokes.

7. Pour into greased muffin tins, filling them two-

thirds full, and bake for 25 minutes.

Banana-Apple Smoothie

Yield: 1 Serving

Ingredients

1/2 banana, peeled & cut into chunks

1/2 cup plain yogurt

1/2 cup unsweetened applesauce

1/4 cup skim milk

1 tablespoon honey

2 tablespoons oat bran

Directions

1. Place banana, yogurt, applesauce, milk, and honey in blender.

2. Blend until smooth.

3. Add oat bran and blend until thickened.

Banana Oat Shake

Yield: 2 Servings

Ingredients

1/2 cup cooked oatmeal, chilled

2/3 cup skim milk

2 tablespoons brown sugar

1 tablespoon wheat germ

1 1/2 teaspoons vanilla extract

1/2 frozen banana, cut into chunks Directions

1. Place oatmeal in blender and blend for a few minutes.

2. Add milk, brown sugar, wheat germ, vanilla, and 1/2 banana. Blend until thick and smooth.

3. Serve with ice if desired.

Chicken and Corn Chowder

Yield: 12 Servings

Ingredients

12 slices bacon, low sodium

2 onions, chopped

7 cups chicken broth, low sodium

4 potatoes, diced and soaked

8 cups Corn

8 boneless chicken breasts, diced

6 tablespoons fresh thyme, chopped

4 cups Mocha Mix

1/2 teaspoon black pepper

8 green onions, chopped

Directions

1. Cook bacon in a pan until crisp, remove bacon and set aside.

2. Saute onions in the bacon fat.

3. Add broth and potatoes.

Cover and simmer for 10 mins.

5. Add corn, chicken and thyme.

6. Cover and simmer until chicken is cooked (15

mins).

7. Stir Mocha Mix into the soup and simmer 2 mins.

8. Sprinkle in bacon, pepper and green onions.

Canned Fish Tacos

Yield: 2 Servings

Ingredients

2 tablespoons chopped onion

2 teaspoons oil

1 can tuna, drained and rinsed

1/2 cup corn, canned or frozen

1/4 cup canned diced tomatoes, no salt added

1/2 teaspoon chili powder

4 corn tortillas

Directions

1. In a frying pan cook onions in oil over medium heat until they turn clear.

2. Add tuna, corn, tomatoes, and chili powder.

3. Cook until heated through, about 3-5 minutes.

4. Serve with warm tortillas. Add sour cream, lettuce, and hot sauce if desired.

Beef Barley Soup

Yield: 10 Servings

Ingredients

1/2 teaspoon black pepper

2 lbs beef stew meat, diced 1 inch cubes

1/4 cup vegetable oil, divided

1 cup chopped onion

1/2 cup sliced mushrooms

2 carrots, diced

1/2 teaspoon garlic, minced

1/4 teaspoon dried thyme

1 can (14.5 ounces) chicken broth, low sodium

3 cups water

1 frozen package (16 ounces) of vegetables

2 potatoes, soaked and diced

1/2 cup barley

Directions

1. Season beef with pepper.

2. Add 2 tablespoons oil to stew pot and saute 5 minutes.

Add 2 more tablespoons of oil and add onions, carrots and mushrooms.

4. Saute for 5 minutes and stir often.

5. Add garlic and thyme and saute for 3 mins.

6. Add chicken broth and water to pot.

7. Add mixed vegtables, potatoes and barley.

8. Stir and bring to boil.

9. Cover and reduce heat.

10.

Simmer 1 to 1 1/2 hours.

Chicken and Dumplings

Yield: 8 Servings

Ingredients

1 whole chicken or 3 lbs chopped chicken

2 cups water or low sodium chicken broth

1 stalk celery with leaves, cut fine

2-3 carrots, sliced

1/2 teaspoon black pepper

1/2 teaspoon mace or nutmeg

1/4 cup flour

2 eggs

2/3 cup milk

3 teaspoons baking powder

2 cups flour

2 tablespoons unsalted butter or margarine

Directions

1. Put chicken, vegetables, spices and water or broth into slow cooker.

2. Add more water, enough to cover chicken by about 1".

Turn cooker on low for about 6-8 hours.

4. Remove the chicken to an ovenproof dish.

5. Remove the bones if you want, they may just fall off.

6. Cover and keep warm.

7. Turn slow cooker up to high heat. Add the 1/4

cup flour and whisk quickly, to avoid lumps.

8. Cut the butter into the 2 cups of flour with two

knives, a pastry cutter or food processor.

9. Blend in wet ingredients to a stiff dough and drop by spoonfuls into the boiling broth.

10. Cover the cooker, reduce the heat to

prevent boiling, and cook for 15 minutes without removing the lid.

11. Put chicken in large serving dish and pour thickened sauce over, serve with dumplings.

Chicken N' Orange Salad Sandwich
Yield: 6 Servings

Ingredients

1 cup chopped cooked chicken

1/2 cup celery, diced

1/2 cup green pepper, chopped

1/4 cup onion, finely sliced

1 cup Mandarin oranges

1/3 cup mayonnaise

Directions

1. Toss chicken, celery, green pepper, and onion to mix.

2. Add mandarin oranges and mayonnaise.

3. Mix gently.

4. Serve on bread.

Chinese Chicken Salad

Yield: 8 Servings

Ingredients

2 packages ramen noodles

3 tablespoons, divided olive oil

2 tablespoons sesame seeds

2 cups cooked chicken or turkey, diced

1/2 head cabbage, shredded and chopped

4 green onions, diced

1/4 cup sugar or Splenda

1 tablespoon sesame oil

1/2 cup white wine vinegar or rice vinegar Directions

1. Take the ramen noodles and smash while still in the packet.

2. Open packages and remove the seasoning packets.

3. Heat 1 tablespoon olive oil in a skillet.

4. Add in the dry noodles and sesame seeds.

Toast until golden brown.

6. Mix chicken or turkey, cabbage, and green onions in a bowl, then add the ramen noodles and sesame seeds.

7. Blend sugar, sesame oil, 2 tablespoons olive oil, and vinegar in a separate bowl.

8. Dress the salad with the dressing.

Cider Cream Chicken

Yield: 8 Servings

Ingredients

4 bone-in chicken breasts

2 tablespoons unsalted butter

3/4 cup apple cider

1/2 cup half and half

Directions

1. Melt butter over medium-high heat. Add chicken and brown on both sides.

2. Add cider and reduce heat to medium; simmer for about 20 minutes.

3. Remove chicken from skillet.

4. Boil cider until reduced to about 1/4 cup.

5. Add half and half over heat; whisk until slightly thickened.

6. Pour cream sauce over chicken and serve.

Cowboy Caviar Bean and Rice Salad
Yield: 6 Servings

Ingredients

1/2 cup fresh or frozen corn, cooked

3 cups rice, cooked

1/4 cup lime juice

1/2 cup olive or canola oil

2 tablespoons brown sugar

1 tablespoon Dijon mustard

1/2 teaspoon black pepper

1/2 cup red bell pepper, diced

1/2 cup low sodium canned black beans, drained and rinsed

1 jalapeño, seeded and diced

1/2 cup cilantro, chopped

Directions

1. Prepare rice and corn, let cool.

To make the dressing whisk lime juice, oil, brown sugar, mustard, and black pepper together.

3. In a large bowl combine all other ingredients.

4. Pour dressing over salad and stir.

5. Chill for one hour in refrigerator.

Fruity Chicken Salad

Yield: 8 Servings

Ingredients

2 cups chicken breasts, cooked and cubed or 12.5 ounces canned chicken

1 cup sliced almonds

1 stalk celery, chopped

1 green onion, chopped

2 cups seedless grapes

1 apple, cubed

3/4 cup raisins

1/2 cup sour cream

1/4 cup mayo

1 teaspoon rice vinegar, unseasoned

2 teaspoons sugar

1/2 teaspoon Chinese Five-Spice Blend

Dialysis Cookbook Directions

1. In a large bowl, mix chicken, almonds, celery, green onion, grapes, apples, and raisins.

2. In a separate bowl combine sour cream, mayo, rice vinegar, sugar, and Chinese Five-Spice

Blend.

3. Mix dressing into chicken mixture.

Low Salt Stir-Fry

Yield: 2 Servings

Ingredients

4 cups (about 3/4 pound) mixed greens (lettuce, collard, beet, etc)

1 tablespoon olive oil

1 cup onions, sliced thin

1/4 teaspoon curry powder

1 tablespoon low sodium soy sauce

1/2 cup white wine vinegar or rice vinegar

8 ounces tofu, cut into cubes

1/2 teaspoon sesame oil

1/2 teaspoon sesame seeds

Directions

1. Cut greens into 2 inch long shreds.

2. Heat oil in wok or saute pan.

3. Saute onions until translucent, about 2 minutes.

4. Sprinkle curry over onions and add sugar and greens.

Cover.

6. Reduce heat and let greens steam in their own juice until tender, 5-8 minutes. (During this time, uncover and turn occasionally. Add a little

water if sticking.) Don't overcook or greens will turn darker.

7. Remove greens with slotted spoon leaving juices in pan.

8. Add soy sauce and vinegar, heat to boiling.

9. When sauce is slightly thickened, remove from heat and poor over greens.

10. Garnish with sesame oil and seeds.

Herb Breaded Chicken

Yield: 4 Servings

Ingredients

1/4 teaspoon basil

1/4 teaspoon thyme

1/4 teaspoon oregano

1/4 teaspoon tarragon

1/4 teaspoon paprika

1/4 teaspoon fresh ground black pepper

1 1/2 slices whole wheat bread

1 pound boneless chicken breasts or 1 1/2 pounds "bone in" chicken Directions

1. Preheat oven to 400 degrees.

2. Combine herbs and spices in blender or food processor with bread.

3. Mix well.

4. Dip chicken in herb mixture.

Bake in a single layer for 20 minutes (boneless chicken) or 50 minutes (bone-in).

Honey Herb Glazed Turkey

Yield: 6-8 Serving

Ingredients

10-12 pounds whole turkey

1 onion, cut into wedges

2 celery stalks, whole

1 lemon, cut into chunks

1/3 cup olive oil

1/2 cup unsalted butter

2 tablespoons fresh sage leaves

1/3 cup fresh thyme stripped from stems (about 14 stems)

2 fresh bay leaves

2 teaspoons celery seed

1/4 cup honey

2 teaspoons lemon juice

Directions

1. Heat oven to 350 degrees.

2. Remove neck and giblets from turkey.

3. Fill bird with onion, celery and lemon.

3 Rub skin with olive oil.

5. Put on 2 sheets of aluminum foil.

6. Cover top of bird with seperate sheet of foil, which you will remove later.

7. Seal the edges of the foil and put on a rack and roast in the oven.

8. While turkey is cooking, melt butter, chop sage

and thyme leaves finely.

9. Add bay leaves, chopped herbs, and honey to

butter.

10. Simmer 10 minutes, until butter is lightly browned, then remove the bay leaves.

11. When the turkey reaches 145-155

degrees, raise oven temperature to 500

degrees, remove top foil and baste turkey with honey herb mixture, every 5-10 minutes or so.

12. Using a thermometer, when the turkey reaches 160 degrees remove from oven, tent with foil and let rest 30 minutes before carving.

Hungarian Goulash

Yield: 6 Servings

Ingredients

2 pounds beef round steak

1/4 cup flour

1/4 cup butter or oil

1 1/2 cups onions, chopped

1 cup low sodium beef stock

2 teaspoons sweet paprika

1 tablespoon red wine or wine vinegar Directions

1. Cut meat into 1 inch cubes and coat with flour.

2. Heat butter or oil in heavy pot and brown meat on both sides.

3. Add onion and saute.

4. Add stock. Add more as needed. It should be thick, stew like consistency but easy to stir.

5. Cover pot.

6. Simmer the meat for 1 1/2 hours.

Remove meat from pot; keep warm.

8. Add paprika to stock and thicken with flour or corn starch.

9. Add wine or vinegar.

10.

Serve goulash with Spaetzle or noodles and salad.

Italian Meatballs

Yield: 12 (2 Meatball Each)

Ingredients

1.5 pounds ground beef

2 large eggs, beaten

1/2 cup dry oatmeal flakes

3 tablespoons parmesan cheese

1/2 tablespoon olive oil

1/2 tablespoon garlic powder

1 teaspoon dried oregano

1/2 cup onion, chopped

1/2 teaspoon black pepper

Directions

1. Preheat oven to 375 degrees.

2. Combine all ingredients in a large bowl and mix together.

3. Roll into 1" balls and place on a baking sheet.

4. Bake for 10 to 15 minutes, until meatballs are cooked through.

To serve, place meatballs in a warming dish or crock pot on low heat setting. Serve with 2 teaspoons sauce on the side. Try our Roasted Red Pepper Sauce for an extra burst of flavor.

Jammin' Jambalaya

Yield: 6 Servings

Ingredients

2 teaspoons olive oil

1/2 pound jumbo shrimp, cooked, tails removed

7 ounces smoked turkey sausage, sliced

1/2 large yellow onion, chopped

1 large red bell pepper, chopped

3 cups collard greens, chopped

2 garlic cloves, minced

1/4 teaspoon cayenne pepper

1/8 teaspoon white pepper

1/4 teaspoon black pepper

1/2 teaspoon dry thyme or 1-2 teaspoons fresh thyme

1/2 teaspoon oregano

2 bay leaves

1/4 teaspoon allspice

1/2 cup rice (white or brown)

1 2/3 cups chicken broth

Dialysis Cookbook Directions

1. Heat olive oil in a large skillet over medium-high heat.

2. Add shrimp, turkey sausage, onion, bell pepper, collards and garlic.

3. Cook for 10 minutes, stirring occasionally.

4. Add remaining ingredients and bring to a boil.

5. Cover, reduce heat to medium-low and simmer for 20 minutes or until rice is tender. (35-40 if using brown rice).

Kickin' Chicken Tacos

Yield: 4 Servings

Ingredients

1 pound boneless, skinless chicken breasts

1 1/2 teaspoons salt-free taco seasoning

1 lime, juiced

8 corn tortillas

1 cup iceberg lettuce, shredded or chopped

1/4 cup sour cream

2 green onions (scallions), sliced

1/2 cup cilantro, chopped

Directions

1. Boil chicken for 20 minutes.

2. Shred chicken into bite-size pieces or chop finely.

3. Toss chicken with Mexican seasoning and lime juice.

4. Fill tortillas with chicken and lettuce.

Top with sour cream, green onions, cilantro or other garnishes.

Lamb Sirloin

Yield: 2 Servings

Ingredients

1 (6 ounce) lamb sirloin

1/4 cup dijon mustard

3/4 cup unseasoned or homeade bread crumbs

2 tablespoons unsalted butter

1 tablespoon fresh rosemary, finely chopped

1 teaspoon dried basil, crumbled

1 clove garlic

Directions

1. Under a broiler or on a barbeque, grill lamb sirloin until halfway done, about 5-7 minutes 2. While meat is cooking, mix herbs with breadcrumbs.

3. Melt butter and add to breadcrumb mixture.

4. Add garlic to mustard, spread on top of the

sirloin.

Sprinkle with breadcrumb mixture, about 1/2 inch thick.

6. Bake at 350 degrees another ten minutes or until the internal temperature is 120 degrees.

7. Serve with a mint sauce or a mint jelly.

Lemon Curry Chicken Salad

Yield: 4 Servings

Ingredients

1/4 cup vegetable oil

1/4 cup frozen lemonade concentrate, thawed

1/4 teaspoon ground ginger

1/4 teaspoon curry powder

1/8 teaspoon garlic powder

1 1/2 cups chicken, cooked and diced

1 1/2 cups grapes, halved

1/2 cup celery, sliced

Directions

1. In a large bowl, whisk together oil, lemonade concentrate, and spices.

2. Add remaining ingredients and toss lightly.

3. Chill at least an hour.

Louisiana BBQ Shrimp

Yield: 15 Servings

Ingredients

 pounds shrimp

2 sticks butter

1 cup olive oil

1/2 cup chili sauce

1/4 cup Worcestershire sauce

2 lemon, thinly sliced

4 garlic cloves, minced

1/4 cup lemon juice

1 tablespoon parsley minced

2 teaspoons paprika

2 teaspoons oregano

2 teaspoons rosemary

3 teaspoons cayenne pepper

1 teaspoon Tabasco sauce

Directions

1. Peel, devein, and wash shrimp.

Combine remaining ingredients in sauce pan.

3. Place over low heat and simmer for 30 minutes.

4. Lightly saute shrimp in olive oil until half cooked.

5. Pour BBQ sauce over shrimp and bring to a light boil.

6. Serve in a bread bowl or a regular bowl with plenty of french bread.

Marinated Shrimp & Pasta Salad
Yield: 10 Servings

Ingredients

12 ounces uncooked tri-color pasta

1/2 large red bell pepper, diced

1/2 large yellow bell pepper, diced

1/2 red onion, diced

4 stalks celery, diced

15-20 baby carrots, thick rounds

1 1/2 cups cauliflower, dime size pieces

1/2 english cucumber, cubed

1/2 pound cooked shrimp

1/4 cup honey

1/4 cup balsamic vinegar

1/2 teaspoon black pepper

1 tablespoon dijon mustard

1/2 teaspoon garlic powder

3/4 cup olive oil

Dialysis Cookbook Directions

1. Cook pasta according to package instructions (rinse and drain under cold water to cool quickly).

2. While pasta is cooking cut up vegetables and put into a large mixing bowl, then add the shrimp.

3. In a small mixing bowl whisk together the

honey, vinegar, black pepper, mustard, and garlic powder.

4. While still whisking, slowly add the oil and whisk everything together.

5. Next add the cooled pasta to the bowl with the

vegetables and shrimp and gently mix it all together.

6. Pour the marinade over the pasta mixture and gently toss for an even coat.

7. Cover with plastic wrap and refrigerate at least 5 hours.

8. Stir and serve chilled.

The King

Mr. Presley himself was well-known for his many talents and quirks. It was known far and wide that Elvis had an interesting favorite sandwich, and we have a great recipe for you to try yourself. Brings new meaning the term "fit for a king".

(Hint: To avoid a soggy or greasy sandwich, take care to drain the bacon grease well. For a sandwich that is a little more "shook up" try using a sharp white cheddar for the cheese and wheat toast.)

Ingredients:
- 2 slices bacon
- 1 tablespoon smooth peanut butter
- 2 slices soft white bread
- 1 slice American cheese
- 1 tablespoon butter, softened

Directions:
1. In a deep, large pan, fry bacon over medium to high heat. Flip bacon as needed to ensure the meat cooks thoroughly. Discard excess grease from the pan and place cooked bacon on dry napkins.
2. Evenly smear the peanut butter over one of the slices of bread. Cover the peanut butter with cheese followed by bacon and top the sandwich with the second bread slice. Butter the entire outside portion of the sandwich and cook in a pan at medium heat. The sandwich is ready after the bread becomes sufficiently browned. Each side should not take more than about 3 minutes to cook.

Veggie Grilled Cheese Sandwich

An easy and delicious way to enjoy the classic grilled cheese.
(Hint: Use butter in place of margarine if desired and the fresh flavor of tomato is a great addition.)
Ingredients:
- 1 1/2 cups coleslaw mix
- 1/2 cup bean sprouts
- 8 thick slices (3/4 inch thick) sourdough bread
- 3 tablespoons margarine, softened
- 3 tablespoons honey mustard
- 6 ounces sliced Havarti cheese

Directions:
1. Combine the sprouts with coleslaw mix in a container.
2. Smear margarine on one side of all bread slices. On the dry side of four bread slices, apply honey mustard. Add a dollop of the sprouts mix to the mustard side and top with Havarti. Complete the sandwiches with the last four slices of bread, ensuring the margarine sides are facing up.
3. Heat your pan on medium and allow the sandwiches to grill until each side is sufficiently browned and cheese has reached a melting point.

Ham and Apple Grilled Cheese

For a simple meal that satisfies your hunger, this recipe may not be the best for a weight loss program but it will give the whole family a tasty serving of protein and fruit.
(Hint: If desired, use your preferred bread or cheese.)
Ingredients:
- 4 slices ham, chopped
- 1 small apple - peeled, cored and finely chopped
- 1 tablespoon mayonnaise
- 2 slices Cheddar cheese
- 4 slices bread
- 2 tablespoons butter
- 2 eggs
- 4 tablespoons milk

Directions:
1. Combine the apple with the meat and mayo in a separate container. Place a dollop of the mixture on two of the bread slices and top each with cheese. Add the remaining bread slices to form the sandwich.
2. Heat a pan at medium level and melt the butter. Mix the milk with the eggs in a separate container. Place the sandwiches in the egg and milk mixture and turn them over. This step should be done quickly to avoid soaking the bread and creating a soggy texture. Cook the sandwiches in the preheated pan until they reach your desired level of

browning on each side. The sandwiches should take about two minutes to cook on each side, ensuring a golden color and a fully cooked egg.

Jalapeno Popper Grilled Cheese Sandwich

For a spicy kick on the classic grilled cheese, enjoy this flavorful recipe. Ciabatta rolls may be breaking the traditional styles of grilled cheese breads, but with its chewy and crunchy texture, may be the perfect fit with this spicy dish.

(Hint: If ciabatta bread is not your preference, we also recommend trying this recipe with sourdough.)

Ingredients:
- 2 ounces cream cheese, softened
- 1 tablespoon sour cream
- 10 pickled jalapeno pepper slices chopped
- 2 ciabatta sandwich rolls
- 4 teaspoons butter
- 8 tortilla chips, crushed
- 1/2 cup shredded Colby-Monterey Jack cheese

Directions:
1. Mix sour cream and jalapeno with the cream cheese, in a container. Heat the pan to medium.
2. Horizontally cut the ciabatta rolls in half, and trim the round tops to create a flat surface. Use 1 tbsp butter on the sliced portion of bottom half, and one tbsp. of butter on the top half. Spread about half the tortilla strips, half the shredded cheese and half the jalapeno mixture on the unbuttered area of the bun bottom. butter on the now flattened top bun.

3. Your sandwiches are ready when all sides are browned and the cheese has reached a melting point.

Grown Up Grilled Cheese Sandwich

A flavorful and more sophisticated sandwich for the adults who still love the comforting flavor of their childhood favorite. With the added flavor components in this recipe, you'll have a restaurant quality sandwich from the comfort of your home.

Ingredients:
- 2 tablespoons butter, divided
- 4 slices whole wheat bread 2 slices white American cheese
- 4 thin slices tomato
- 1/2 avocado, thinly sliced
- 2 tablespoons chopped fresh basil
- 1 teaspoon red pepper flakes
- 1 pinch garlic salt, or to taste
- 4 ounces fresh mozzarella cheese, thinly sliced
- 2 slices provolone cheese

Directions:
1. Heat your pan to medium. Use 1/2 tbsp of butter to evenly cover the side of every bread slice. Buttered side facing outward, place cheese slice, two avocado slices, and two tomato slices each onto two slices of bread.
2. Use your desired amount of pepper flakes, garlic salt and basil leaves over the avocado.
3. Finally, top each sandwich with one provolone slice and about half of the mozzarella. Cover each

sandwich with the last two bread slices, butter side out.
4. Place in heated pan and cook until bread reaches your desired color and cheese reaches your desired consistency.

Sneaky Grilled Cheese Sandwich

Some of us find the best method of eating a serving of vegetables is when you combine them with an old favorite. Without compromising flavor, this meal contains a portion of vegetables and just a small kick of spice.

(Hint: Experiment with the vegetables you love. This recipe is perfect for sneaking servings of vegetables to children. The jalapeno can be left out for a milder flavor, if desired.)

Ingredients:
- 2 slices bread
- 2 slices Cheddar cheese
- 1/4 cup chopped broccoli
- 1/4 cup chopped zucchini
- 1/4 cup chopped green bell pepper
- 1 tablespoon chopped jalapeno pepper
- 3 tablespoons butter

Directions:
1. With bread spread on your countertop or work space, place cheese atop one slice of bread. Add zucchini, bell pepper, broccoli and jalapeno in layers. Add the remaining bread to the top to create the sandwich.
2. With a pan heated to medium/high, allow 1 1/2 tbsp butter to melt. Place sandwich in the pan and cover. Bread will brown within 1 minute. Turn sandwich over adding the last of the butter, and

continue to cook until the second side is browned. This should only take about 1 more minute.

Ham and Broccoli Grilled Cheese

This sandwich is sure to satisfy your hunger with a serving of vegetables, protein and two types of cheese.

Ingredients:
- 2 slices whole grain bread
- 1/4 cup sharp cheddar cheese, grated
- 1/4 cup grated parmesan cheese
- 1/4 cup diced cooked ham*
- 10 small broccoli florets, steamed then diced
- 1/8 teaspoon garlic powder
- Salt, to taste
- Freshly ground black pepper, to taste
- 1 tablespoon olive oil, divided

Directions:
1. In a container, combine the cheeses, broccoli, ham, and spices.
2. Spread the cheese mix over a single piece of bread and top with the second piece of bread.
3. Heat your skillet on medium and use 1/2 tbsp of olive oil to grease the bottom, ensuring an even coat of oil. Promptly set the sandwich into the skillet and cover. Allow the sandwich to cook covered for up to 3 minutes while the bottom browns.
4. Using a spatula, remove sandwich from the skillet. Pour the last of the olive oil into the pan and coat the skillet once again.
5. Flip your sandwich back into the skillet and cover again. Allow the sandwich to cook covered until the

second side is browned. This should take another 2 or 3 minutes. Enjoy promptly after cooking.

Grilled cheese with apple and cinnamon

This surprising combination is a delicious light yet plentiful option. Perfect for a lazy lunch.
(Hint: Green apples and whole wheat bread are a delicious recommendation and cheddar cheese adds a delicious contrast to the tart apple slices.)

Ingredients:
- 1 tablespoon softened butter
- 2 slices white bread
- 1 small apple - peeled, cored, and sliced
- 1/2 teaspoon ground cinnamon
- 1 slice American cheese

Directions:
1. Heat pan over medium. Butter all slices of bread on one side. Layer sliced apples on the plain side of the bread and add a pinch of cinnamon.
2. Next add a layer of cheese.
3. Last, cover the sandwich with the second piece of bread with butter side out. Place the sandwich into the pan and grill each side until browned (about 3 minutes for each side.)

Grilled Cheese with Tomato, Peppers and Basil

The fresh tomato and basil in this recipe will give you the familiar flavors of the classic grilled cheese and tomato soup combination without the need for a bowl.

Ingredients:
- 8 (1 ounce) slices of bread
- 4 slices Cheddar cheese
- 1 large tomato, sliced
- 2 serrano peppers, seeded and thinly sliced
- 2 teaspoons dried basil salt and pepper to taste
- 2 tablespoons butter

Directions:
1. Evenly coat one side off each of the bread slices with butter. Over medium heat, place 4 slices of bread into a pan with the buttered side facing down.
2. On all of the four bread slices, layer 1 slice of tomato, some serrano pepper, and one slice of cheese. Add spices to your taste preference. Lastly, add the remaining bread to the tops of the sandwiches, with the buttered side facing up.
3. Allow sandwiches to cook until browned. (About 3 minutes for each side.)

Pepper jack, avocado, bacon sandwich

A unique flavor combination that really strays from the original sandwich, you'll love this game changer.
(Hint: Vegetarians enjoy the flavors of this sandwich even without the bacon. Try it both ways! You can also use caramelized onion as a substitute for the onion.)

Ingredients:
- 8 (3/4 inch thick) slices sourdough bread
- 1/4 cup butter
- 8 slices cooked thick bacon
- 8 slices pepper jack cheese
- 1 red onion, sliced into rings
- 1 avocado, halved and cut into
- 1/4-inch slices

Directions:
1. With bread arranged on your counter or workspace, evenly coat all bread slices on one side with butter.
2. Use one cheese slice, onions, the bacon, and avocado to create layers on the unbuttered portion of bread. Top the sandwiches with remaining slices of sourdough.
3. Heat pan over medium and allow sandwiches to cook until each side is browned.

Grilled Cheese with avocado and fruit glaze

This sweet and creamy sandwich pairs deliciously with the warm crunchy toast.

Ingredients:
- 1 ripe avocado, peeled, pitted and cubed
- 2 tablespoons mango jam
- 1 teaspoon fresh lemon juice
- 1 tablespoon minced red onion
- Salt and black pepper to taste
- 2 tablespoons butter with canola oil
- 2 teaspoons Dijon mustard
- 4 slices country white bread
- 4 slices Monterey Jack cheese

Directions:
1. Slice avocado into cubes and place them in a bowl. Heat the jam in the microwave or on stovetop until it is thoroughly warm and has a thin consistency. Mix the jam with the avocado and gently incorporate the onion, lemon juice and spices. In a separate container, combine the oil, butter and mustard and mix until smooth. Evenly coat bread with mustard sauce on one side.
2. On the dry side of the bread, place cheese and about half the avocado and jam mixture. Be sure the avocado and jam mixture is spread evenly.

Lastly, complete the sandwich with the remaining bread with the butter side facing up.
3. With a pan heated over medium, set the sandwiches inside and allow to cook about 3 minutes until browned and slightly crunchy.

Dulce de Leche Grilled Cheese

This delicious dessert-like sandwich is a sweet, indulgent treat that is perfect for a midnight snack. Dulce de Leche can be made by allowing sugar and milk to cook down to a caramel-like spread. You can also purchase Dulce de Leche at stores that offer Hispanic ingredients.

Ingredients:
- 1/4 cup cream cheese, softened
- 1 tablespoon dulce de leche (milk caramel spread)
- 1/2 teaspoon ground cinnamon
- 4 slices cinnamon-raisin bread
- 1 small apple - peeled, cored and thinly sliced

Directions:
1. Combine the dulce de leche with the cinnamon and cream cheese. Evenly coat two bread slices with this spread. Layer the apples evenly over cream cheese mixture. Be sure to save enough apple for both sandwiches. Place the last two bread slices atop the sandwiches.
2. Oil your pan with a cooking spray of your choice and heat the pan over medium. Let the sandwiches cook until browned on both sides.

Cinnamon apple deluxe

The sweet and savory flavor is sure to be a crowd pleaser. This recipe is perfect around the holidays when you may have many of these ingredients leftover in your refrigerator.
(Hint: Roll the sandwiches in the milk and eggs quickly to avoid a soggy texture.)

Ingredients:
- 2 purchased cinnamon buns
- 4 slices aged Cheddar cheese, divided
- 4 slices Brie cheese, divided
- 4 slices deli ham, shredded (divided)
- 1 small apple - peeled, cored, and sliced (divided)
- 2 tablespoons butter
- 2 eggs
- 1/4 cup milk

Directions:
1. Cut the pastries in half, and set up your workspace. For best results, there is a specific method to layering your ingredients. On the bottom of the pastry place the slice of cheddar, then the brie slice, followed by the apple slices and ham, followed by a second brie slice, a second cheddar slice and the top half of the pastry.
2. Heat your pan over medium and melt the butter. In a separate bowl, mix the milk and eggs.

3. Roll the sandwich into the milk and egg mix and cook the sandwiches in the heated pan until browned.

Pico De Gallo Grilled Cheese Sandwich

This sandwich does not contain meat but packs a lot of flavor. A unique and tasty way to use leftover Mexican food for an easy lunch.

Ingredients:
- 1 tomato, diced
- 1/2 white onion, diced
- 2 tablespoons chopped fresh cilantro, or to taste (optional)
- 1/2 lime, juiced
- salt and ground black pepper to taste

Sandwich:

- 3 tablespoons softened butter, or as needed
- 10 slices white bread
- 10 slices provolone cheese

Directions:
1. Prepare onion, tomato, lime juice and cilantro in a container.
2. Butter all bread slices on one side. With buttered side facing down, set up your work space. Place provolone onto each slice and add a generous dollop of pico de gallo to five of the cheese bread slices. Place the remaining cheese bread slices atop the pico de gallo slices.

3. Place your pan at medium heat. Cook the sandwiches until the outsides are browned.

Grilled Hawaiians

If you like Hawaiian pizza, this is the perfect sandwich for you. The sweet and tangy pineapple, with the salty ham is a familiar flavor combined to make a delicious sandwich.

Ingredients:
- 3 tablespoons butter or margarine, softened
- 8 slices bread
- 4 slices Swiss cheese
- 8 slices thinly sliced cooked ham
- 1 (8 ounce) can crushed pineapple, drained

Directions:
1. Preheat your pan over medium. Butter each of the bread slices on one side.
2. Lay 4 bread slices onto the pan, with the buttered side facing down. Lay a cheese slice, two tbsp. of pineapple and two pieces of ham on each of the bread slices.
3. Top the sandwiches with the rest of the bread slices ensuring the buttered side of the bread is facing up. When the sandwiches are browned, turn them over and cook the opposite side.

SPAM, Tomato, Cheddar Cheese, and Sweet Onion Sandwiches

With or without the SPAM, this is a comforting sandwich with a unique flavor. The best part is you probably have all the ingredients already!

Ingredients:
- 1/4 cup spicy brown mustard
- 8 slices whole wheat bread
- 1 (12 ounce) can fully cooked luncheon meat (SPAM), cut into
- 1/4 inch slices
- 8 slices Cheddar cheese
- 2 large tomatoes, cut into 1/2-inch slices
- 1 sweet onion, thinly sliced
- 1/4 cup softened butter

Directions:
1. Coat the slices of bread on one side with mustard. Arrange the meat onto four of the slices of bread and place tomato, onion and two slices of cheese atop the meat slices. Top the sandwiches with the other four slices of bread with the dry side facing up. Butter the outer areas of all sandwiches.
2. Set your sandwiches in a pan heated over low-medium and pan-fry each side until browned and slightly crunchy. This may take up to 6 minutes for each side.

Grilled Mushroom and Swiss

This combination is a popular choice in the hamburger world, so we tried it at home with a bit of a twist. You will not be disappointed!

(Hint: Mozzarella works as a replacement for Swiss and for extra flavor, try adding onion or garlic to your mushrooms!)

Ingredients:
- 1 tablespoon extra-virgin olive oil
- 1/4 cup baby spinach (optional)
- 1/4 cup sliced fresh mushrooms salt and ground black pepper to taste
- 2 slices bread
- 1 tablespoon softened butter
- 2 slices Swiss cheese

Directions:
1. Over medium, warm the oil in your pan and add the spinach, mushroom, and desired spices. Stir the vegetables while they cook. When the vegetables are ready, the spinach should have shrunk significantly, and the mushrooms should be tender when pierced with a fork. Set your vegetables in a separate container to await the next step.
2. Butter all bread slices on one side. With the dry side facing up, lay one piece of your bread in the skillet. Layer the cheese and the mushroom mix before topping the sandwich with a remaining slice of bread. The butter side of the bread should be facing

up. Allow the sandwich to cook on each side until they are sufficiently brown in color.

Turkey and Feta Grilled Sandwich

For a delicious meal that pleases everyone, whip up a few of these simple crowd pleasers.

(Hint: Add your favorite vegetables or meat for a delightful twist. This sandwich works well with a side of fresh fruit or French fries.)

Ingredients:

- 2 slices smoked deli turkey
- 2 slices wheat bread
- 2 leaves lettuce
- 1 1/2 tablespoons crumbled feta cheese
- 1 tablespoon Italian salad dressing
- 1 tablespoon butter

Directions:

1. On your first slice of bread, place turkey, feta and lettuce. Use a butter knife to coat the second slice of bread with the salad dressing. Cover the sandwich with the second slice of bread with the dry side facing up.
2. Over medium, place the butter in your pan and allow it to melt. Grill your sandwich in the butter until each side is sufficiently brown in color.

Brie and Pear Sandwich

This fancy sounding sandwich is easy to make and sure to impress the vegetarians in your life. Don't be fooled, this will be well-received by everyone at your table!

Ingredients:
- 2 tablespoons butter, softened
- 2 thick slices French bread
- 6 thin slices Brie cheese, or more to taste
- 12 fresh thyme leaves, or to taste
- 1 pinch cracked black pepper
- 6 slices pear (such as Bosc)
- salt to taste

Directions:
1. Coat your bread slices with butter on one side. Be sure they are well coated with butter.
2. On medium, allow your pan to heat and lay the sliced bread with the dry side facing up. Layer the cheese with your desired seasonings.
3. On one of the bread slices, layer the slices of pear atop the cheese and sprinkle with a dash of salt.
4. Using a spatula, turn the first bread slice onto the bread slice layered with pears. Allow the sandwich to cook until thoroughly heated. Your sandwich is ready when the cheese has reached a melting point, and the pears have been warmed.

Turkey and swiss Sandwich

This is an easy and tasty way to utilize your Thanksgiving leftovers.

(Hint: You can enjoy this sandwich pan-fried or broiled as a turkey melt. Experiment with your favorite ingredients such as fresh vegetables.)

Ingredients:
- 1 tablespoon mayonnaise
- 2 slices thick-cut rye bread
- 2 slices Swiss cheese
- 2 slices leftover turkey meat, or to taste
- 1/4 cup baby spinach, or to taste

Directions:
1. Set your oven to the broil setting. Place the rack above the heat, about 6 in.
2. Cover one side of the bread slices with mayo. Add turkey, spinach and cheese atop the mayo-side of one slice of bread. Cover the sandwich with the remaining slice of bread. Set the sandwich on an oven-safe dish.
3. Allow the sandwich to cook on the broil setting until the cheese is melted and bubbling.

Grilled Camembert Sandwich

An easy way to impress your visitors or treat yourself.

Ingredients:
- 2 ounces Camembert cheese
- 2 thick slices white bread
- 1 tablespoon whole cranberry sauce
- 1 dash balsamic vinegar
- 1 tablespoon butter, softened

Directions:
1. Use a butter knife to thoroughly cover one bread slice with the cheese. Cover the cheese layer with the cranberry sauce and top with a light sprinkle of vinegar. Last, use the second piece of bread to complete the sandwich and butter the outside areas of the entire sandwich.
2. Grill your sandwich on medium heat in a pan until lightly browned on each side. Serve promptly while it's fresh from the griddle.

Roasted Red Pepper and Ham Sandwich

Roasted to perfection! Try using chipotle mayo to spice it up even more! Your family will love this tasty sandwich.

Ingredients:
- 2 teaspoons mayonnaise
- 2 slices sourdough bread
- 2 slices provolone cheese
- 2 thin slices ham
- 1/2 roasted red pepper packed in oil, drained and sliced
- 2 teaspoons butter
- 2 teaspoons grated Parmesan or Romano cheese

Directions:
1. Using a butter knife, evenly coat one side of all bread slices. Layer a slice of cheese, peppers, ham and a second cheese slice on one bread slice. Complete the sandwich with a second bread slice, mayo-side down. Spread butter along the outer portion of the sandwich then top with a dash of the grated cheese.
2. Over medium, grill the sandwich in a pan until both sides are browned and the cheese has reached a melting point.

Grilled Peanut Butter and Banana Sandwich

This warm and nutritious breakfast or snack idea is sure to hit the spot.

Ingredients:
- cooking spray
- 2 tablespoons peanut butter
- 2 slices whole wheat bread
- 1 banana, sliced

Directions:
1. Allow pan to heat over medium, and spray with a non-stick baking oil.
2. Using a butter knife, cover the bread slices with peanut butter on one side.
3. Layers sliced bananas over the peanut butter and complete the sandwich with the second bread slice.
4. Cook each side until the bread is lightly browned and the peanut butter and banana are warm.

Turkey Reuben Sandwiches

These simple and delicious sandwiches are a popular twist on the original New York favorite.

(Hint: Marble rye is not for everyone, you may substitute a deli rye or Jewish rye for a less intense caraway flavor.)

Ingredients:
- 1 cup sauerkraut, drained
- 10 ounces sliced deli turkey meat
- 2 tablespoons butter
- 4 slices marble rye bread
- 4 slices Swiss cheese
- 4 tablespoons thousand island salad dressing, or to taste

Directions:
1. Thoroughly butter all slices of bread on one side and cover the second side with the salad dressing. You may want to heat your meat and sauerkraut on the stove or in a microwave at this time.
2. Place an even portion of turkey, cheese and sauerkraut on two bread slices ensuring the buttered side is face down. Cover the sandwich with the third and fourth bread slices ensuring the butter is facing up.
3. At low-medium setting, place the sandwiches in a pan and allow to cook until sufficiently browned on both sides.

Chicken Cordon Bleu Sandwich

Another way to easily and deliciously utilize your leftover food, enjoy this interesting take on two classic meals.

Ingredients:
- 2 slices bread
- 2 tablespoons margarine, divided
- 2 slices Swiss cheese
- 1 cooked chicken breast half
- 1 tablespoon barbecue sauce
- 2 slices honey-cured deli ham

Directions:
1. Use a butter knife to add margarine to all bread slices on one side. With the dry side facing up, lay the bread into a pan heated over medium.
2. Layer a cheese slice, barbecue sauce, chicken, ham and the second cheese slice atop the bread in the pan. Use the second slice of bread to complete the sandwich, with the margarine side facing up.
3. Lightly grill the sandwich, until cheese reaches your desired consistency and the bread is browned on each side.

Amazing Whisky Grilled Baby Back Ribs Recipe

Ingredients

2 (2 pound) slabs baby back pork ribs
1 pinch coarsely ground black pepper
1 tablespoon ground red chile pepper
2 1/4 tablespoons vegetable oil
1/2 cup minced onions
1 1/2 cups water
1/2 cup tomato paste
1/2 cup white vinegar
1/2 cup brown sugar
2 1/2 tablespoons honey
2 tablespoons Worcestershire sauce
2 teaspoons salt
1/4 teaspoon coarsely ground black pepper
1 1/4 teaspoons liquid smoke flavoring
2 teaspoons whiskey
2 teaspoons garlic powder
1/4 teaspoon paprika
1/2 teaspoon onion powder
1 tablespoon dark molasses
1/2 tablespoon ground red chile pepper

Directions

Step 1 Preheat oven to 300 degree F (150 degrees C).
Advertisement
Step 2 Cut each full rack of steak by 50 %, so that you have 4 half racks. Sprinkle salt and pepper (more pepper than salt), and you tablespoon chile cayenne pepper over meat. Place each half tray in aluminum foil. Bake for 2 1/2 hours.
3 Meanwhile, heat olive oil in a medium saucepan over medium heat. Cook and stir the onions in oil for 5 minutes. Blend in water, tomato paste, vinegar, dark brown sugar, honey, and Worcestershire sauce. Season with 2 tablespoon salt, 1/4 teaspoon black pepper, liquefied smoke, whiskey, garlic clove powder, paprika, red onion powder, dark molasses, and 1/2 tablespoon ground chile pepper. Bring mixture to a boil, then reduce heat. Simmer for 1/4 several hours, uncovered, or until sauce thickens. Take away from heat, and set sauce apart.
Step 4 Preheat an outside grill for high heat.
Step five Remove the steak from the oven, and enable stand twelve minutes. Take away the wine racks from the foil, and place on the grill. Barbeque grill the ribs for 3 to 4 minutes on each aspect. Brush sauce on the ribs while they're grilling, just before you serve them (adding it too early will burn it).

Baby Back Ribs with Espresso Barbecue Sauce

Ingredients

2 racks baby back ribs (about 4 to 6 ribs per person)
salt Grey salt
black pepper Freshly ground black pepper
espresso Espresso Sauce recipe follows
4 tablespoons garlic mashed and minced garlic
4 tablespoons olive oil extra-virgin olive oil
1 cup cider vinegar cider vinegar
1/2 cup soy sauce soy sauce
2 cups ketchup ketchup
2 cups honey honey
salt Grey salt
2 cups espresso demitasse espresso (or about 1/2 cup of strong coffee or instant espresso)

Directions

Preheat oven to 325 degrees F.

Minimize each rack of ribs in half over the bone thus they can easily be stacked. Lay these people out on the parchment paper in which these were wrapped for easy cleaning.

Salt and cayenne pepper liberally on both sides and pat seasonings into the meats. Be sure to over time of year the ribs, because area of the rub will certainly inevitably come away in the pan. About a cookie sheet lined with aluminum foil, stack the ribs close to one another, regarding 3 layers high. Place in the oven for 2 hours, shifting the underlying part layer of steak for the top just about every half an hour until that they are tender and almost falling away the bone.

A single half hour before serving, transfer steak to a preheated grill (if employing coals, make sure they may have burnt straight down to an ember). Brush ribs with Espresso Sauce and close grill. Continue to turn and brush the steak with sauce every 10 minutes, regarding 3 more occasions.

Fresh ground dark self defense

Mash garlic herb together with the side of a knife and then mince carefully to release natural oils.

Add olive olive oil to a preheated saute pan. Put the garlic and saute until this gets light dark brown, about 1 small. Add cider apple cider vinegar, soy sauce, ketchup, and honey and stir well. Increase a pinch of grey salt, after that whisk in the caffeine. Add freshly surface black pepper, to taste. Provide a simmer and simmer for 5 minutes.

Let cool and shop in refrigerator to get up to a couple of weeks.

Baby Back Ribs with Spicy Peach BBQ Sauce

Ingredients

2 tablespoons light brown sugar
1 tablespoon kosher salt
2 teaspoons smoked paprika
2 racks pork baby back ribs (about 5 pounds total), membrane removed
1 tablespoon extra-virgin olive oil
1 small onion, diced
1 clove garlic, chopped
one 3-inch piece ginger, peeled and chopped
ounce one 10- bag frozen peaches, thawed
3/4 cup apple cider vinegar
1/2 cup packed light brown sugar
1/2 teaspoon kosher salt
1/2 teaspoon calabrian chili paste

Directions

Intended for the ribs: Preheat the oven to 300 degrees Farrenheit.

In a little bowl, mix together the sugar, salt and paprika. Place the ribs on 2 sheets of aluminium foil large enough to wrap around them and seal off. Rub the steak evenly on the sides with the glucose mixture. Bring the foil up and around the ribs and crimp shut down. Place on a rimmed baking bed sheet. Bake until tender but not disintegrating, about 3 1/2 hours. Allow to cool slightly, about 30 minutes.

For the sauce: Temperature a medium saucepan over medium temperature. Add the oil, onion, garlic and ginger to the pan and cook, stirring often with a wooden tea spoon, until the onions are soft and fragrant, about 4 minutes. Add the peaches and mix to coat with the flavors. Put the vinegar, sugar, salt and Calabrian chili and blend to combine. Bring to a simmer, then decrease the temperature to low to maintain a mild simmer. Add any dripping that may have accumulated on the sheet pan from the pork. Simmer until the peaches are extremely soft, about 30 minutes. Applying an immersion food blender, puree the spices until it finally is as smooth or as big as you like.

Preheat the broiler to high heat. Tea spoon one-quarter of the sauce throughout the ribs. Broil for 4 minutes. Remove and repeat the process another 2 times, until the marinade is thick, sticky and golden brown. Serve with more sauce on the side if desired.

Baked BBQ Baby Back Ribs

Ingredients

1/2 cup chile powder ancho chile powder
1/4 cup sugar white sugar
1/4 cup brown sugar brown sugar
1/4 cup salt salt
2 tablespoons black pepper freshly ground black pepper
1 tablespoon cumin ground cumin
1 teaspoon dry mustard dry mustard
1 teaspoon cayenne pepper ground cayenne pepper
1/2 teaspoon pepper ground dried chipotle pepper
1 rack pork ribs baby back pork ribs
1 cup sauces barbeque sauce

Directions

The first step Preheat oven to 250 degrees F (120 degrees C). Advertisement

Step 2 Mix ancho republic of chile powder, white sugar, brown-sugar, salt, dark-colored pepper, cumin, dry out mustard, cayenne pepper, and chipotle self defense in a small bowl until combined.

Step 3 Place steak meat-side down on aluminum foil. Prick back of rib tray many times with a knife.

Step four Amply apply coating of dry rub to all sides of rib rack.

Step five With rib rack meat-side down, flip foil around it to create a tight seal. Transfer to sheet baking pan.

Step 6 Cook in preheated oven until tender and cooked through, about 2 hours. Take out and cool 15 minutes.

Step seven Rise oven temperature to 350 degrees Farreneheit (175 degrees C).

Step 8 Open up foil, drain and discard any accumulated juices and fat. Brush barbeque marinade on every side of tray.

Step 9 Place rack meat-side up and come back to the oven, leaving foil open up. Bake for twelve minutes, remove from oven, and remember to brush another layer of barbeque sauce on meat-side only. Duplicate baking and scrubbing with sauce some more times, to get a total of 50 minutes baking period.

Step 10 Lower rack into specific rib segments and serve with even more barbeque sauce.

Barbecue Chicken Recipe

Ingredients

1 whole chicken, into halves
1/4 cup rice vinegar
2 tablespoons barbeque sauces
2 cloves garlic, crushed
1 tablespoon salt
1 teaspoon ground black pepper
1 teaspoon paprika
1 teaspoon onion powder
1/2 teaspoon cayenne pepper
1/2 cup barbeque sauces, or as needed

Directions

The first step Cut 1/2-inch profound slashes in the skin-side of each chicken half; 2 cuts in each breast, 2 in the thigh, and 1 on the leg; remove side tips.
Advertisement
Stage 2 Whisk rice vinegar, barbeque marinade, and garlic jointly in large pan. Place chicken in bowl and be to coat chicken in the marinade. Organise chicken halves, cut-side down, in the bottom of the marinade

bowl, cover the bowl with plastic wrap, and refrigerate for one hour.

Step 3 Preset the a backyard grill for medium-high heat and lightly oil the grate.

Step 4 Take away chicken from dish, pat chicken dry out with paper-towels, and discard marinade. Place chicken halves, skin-side up, on a platter and season with salt, pepper, paprika, onion powder, and cayenne pepper.

Step five Cook chicken, skin-side down, on the preheated grill for three to four minutes. Switch chicken over, close the lid of the grill, and cook, basting with remaining barbeque sauce ever 6 minutes, until no much longer pink at the bone and the juices run clear, about 35 minutes. An instant-read thermometer inserted into the thicker part of the thigh, nearby the bone should read one hundred sixty five degrees F (74 degrees C).

Barbecue Ribs with Gochujang Sauce

Ingredients

2 racks baby back pork ribs (about 2 pounds each)
kosher salt, freshly ground pepper
4 scallions, cut into 1-inch pieces
10 garlic cloves, peeled
1 3-inch piece peeled ginger, very coarsely chopped
2 tablespoons vegetable oil, plus more for grill
3/4 cup gochujang (korean hot pepper paste)
1/2 cup ketchup
1/3 cup fresh lime juice
3 tablespoons plum sauces
2 tablespoons light brown sugar
1 tablespoon fish sauces
1 tablespoon soy sauce
lime wedges, for serving

Directions

Preheat oven to 300°. Pat ribs dry; season generously on both sides with salt and pepper. Wrap each rack in a double layer of foil, crimping edges tightly, and place on a rimmed baking sheet. Bake until meat yields easily when pierced with a skewer but is not quite falling off the bone, 2–2 1/2 hours. Remove from oven and let sit inside foil until cool enough to handle.

Preset the oven to 300°. Pat ribs dry out; season generously about both sides with salt and pepper. Wrap each stand in a double level of foil, crimping edges tightly, and place over a rimmed baking sheet. Bake until meat makes easily when punctured with a skewer although not really slipping off the bone tissue, 2–2 1/2 several hours. Remove from the oven and let stay inside foil right up until cool enough to handle.

Meanwhile, pulse scallions, garlic, and turmeric in a food processor until finely chopped. Heat 2 Tbsp. oil in a medium saucepan over medium. Put aromatics and make meals, stirring frequently , right up until softened, golden, and starting to adhere to bottom of skillet, about 4 mins. Add gochujang, ketchup, lime juice, bonbon sauce, sugar, seafood sauce, soy sauce, and 1/4 cup water and blend until smooth. Bring to a simmer and cook, stir often to stop scorching, until thick, 5–10 minutes. Take away sauce from temperature; season with sodium.

Prepare a barbeque grill for medium-high heat; lightly oil grates. Remove ribs by foil (if wanted, stir cooking liquefied into sauce) and cut racks in half crosswise. Place ribs on barbeque grill, meaty side straight down, and grill right up until lightly charred, regarding 1 minute. Comb ribs with marinade and turn more than. Brush with even more sauce and continue to grill, turning ribs one or perhaps two more instances, until sauce is lightly charred found in spots, about 2 minutes. Transfer to a cutting panel and let others 5 mins before cutting into individual steak.

Serve ribs with remaining sauce and lime we

Meanwhile, pulse scallions, garlic, and ginger in a food processor until finely chopped. Heat 2 Tbsp. oil in a medium saucepan over medium. Add aromatics and cook, stirring often, until softened, golden, and starting to stick to bottom of pan, about 4 minutes. Add gochujang, ketchup, lime juice, plum sauce, sugar, fish sauce, soy sauce, and 1/4 cup water and stir until smooth. Bring to a simmer and cook, stirring often to prevent scorching, until thick, 5–10 minutes. Remove sauce from heat; season with salt.

Prepare a grill for medium-high heat; lightly oil grates. Remove ribs from foil (if desired, stir cooking liquid into sauce) and cut racks in half crosswise. Place ribs on grill, meaty side down, and grill until lightly charred, about 1 minute. Brush ribs with sauce and turn over. Brush with more sauce and continue to grill, turning ribs one or two more times, until sauce is lightly charred in spots, about 2 minutes. Transfer to a cutting board and let rest 5 minutes before slicing into individual ribs.

Serve ribs with remaining sauce and lime wedges.

Barbecue St. Louis Pork Ribs

Ingredients

2 teaspoons paprika
1 1/2 teaspoons whole black peppercorns
1 teaspoon coriander seeds
1 teaspoon cumin seeds
1 teaspoon garlic powder
1 teaspoon onion powder
1/4 teaspoon freshly grated nutmeg
1/4 teaspoon cayenne pepper
3 slabs st. louis style ribs, 2 to 3 pounds each
4 tablespoons kosher salt
1/3 cup spicy brown mustard
special equipment: smoker and 4 ounces hickory or oak wood chunks or chips

Directions

Established a smoker to 225 degrees F.

Combine the paprika, black peppercorns, coriander seeds, cumin seed, garlic powder, onion powder, nutmeg and cayenne in a spice grinder. Method until a great powder is formed, roughly 30 seconds.

Terry the ribs dry out and turn bone-side up. Trim excessive fat and, in the event one conclusion of the ribs is particularly narrow, trim various meats and bone to make certain even cooking. Eliminate the membrane on the underside of the ribs by putting a rounded utensil, an upside-down place works well, between the membrane and the meat at a single ending of the slab. Carefully job the spoon beneath the membrane to loosen but not really tear. Once enough continues to be loosened, use a paper towel to hold on the membrane because you slowly pull it down the piece to remove.

Sprinkle the ribs on equally sides with the salt and brush equally sides with the mustard. Sprinkle two-thirds in the spice blend within the meat side of the ribs and the remaining next on the bone side.

Once the smoker has contacted 225 degrees F, add the solid wood chips or pieces plus the ribs to the smoker.

Smoking for 4 to 5 hours after that test for doneness. There are four conditions that will need to be met for ribs to be done. First, the internal temperature of the meat must be 185 to one hundred ninety degrees F. Second, pick up each slab from the center with tongs and it may suspend into a u-shape and crack a bit. Third, while keeping with the tongs, and bouncing gently, the top of ribs will need to crack slightly. Finally, the meat should pull easily away the bone nevertheless not fall off. If ribs move all tests, take away them through the cigarette smoker and wrap in heavy-duty foil and rest for 12-15 minutes. If certainly not, continue smoking to get 45 minutes to 1 hour and test again until done.

Barbecued Chicken on the Grill

Ingredients

4 pounds of your favorite chicken parts (legs, thighs, wings, breasts), skin-on
salt
extra virgin olive oil or vegetable oil
1 cup barbecue sauces, store-bought or homemade

Directions

1 Oil and salt chicken pieces: Coat the chicken breast pieces with essential olive oil and sprinkle sodium over them upon all sides. a couple of Prepare grill: Put together one side of your grill for high, direct heat. In the event you are employing charcoal or solid wood, make sure there exists a cool side for the grill where there are few to no coals. three or more Sear chicken about hot side of grill, move to cool side: Lay down the chicken pieces skin side straight down on the best side of the grill to be able to sear the skin aspect well. Grill revealed for 5-10 mins, according to how warm the grill is (you do certainly not want the poultry to burn). Once

you have a good sear on a single side, turn the chicken pieces above and move these people to the much cooler side of the grill. If you are by using a gas grill, maintain the flame on only one side of the grill, and move the chicken breast pieces to the cooler side, certainly not directly above the fire. Reduce the temporary to low or medium low (between 250°F and 275°F, no more than 300°F). Cover the grill and make undisturbed for over 20 minutes. 4 Switch over and pan with barbecue spices: Turn the chicken pieces over and baste them with your favorite barbecue spices. Cover the grill again and let to cook another fifteen minutes. Repeat, making the chicken parts over, basting these people with sauce, masking, and cooking another 10-30 minutes. Be aware that timing will count on your grill set-up, the size of your chicken parts, and how cold your chicken pieces are to begin with! If you happen to be grilling smaller items of chicken over a charcoal grill, they might be done much before. The goal is always to maintain a low enough grill temp in order that the poultry cooks "low and slow". 5 End using a sear or perhaps remove from heat when done: The chicken is completed when the internal temperature of the chicken pieces will be 160°F for breasts and 170°F to get thighs, when analyzed using a meat thermometer. Or if you insert the tip of a knife in the middle of the thickest piece and the juices ought to run clear, the chicken is carried out. In case the chicken basically done, turn the pieces over and continue to prepare at a low temperature. If you want, you can finish with a sear within the sizzling side in the barbeque grill. To do this kind of, position the pieces, epidermis side down, in the hot part of the barbeque. Allow them to sear and blacken slightly to get a tiny or two. six Paint with even more barbecue sauce to serve.

Barbecued Seitan Ribz (Vegan Ribs)

Ingredients

1 cup vital wheat gluten
2 tablespoons nutritional yeast
2 teaspoons smoked spanish paprika
2 teaspoons onion powder
1 teaspoon garlic powder
3/4 cup water
2 tablespoons tahini or other nut butter
1 tablespoon soy sauce
1 teaspoon liquid smoke
1 cup about of your favorite barbecue sauces see some suggestions below

Directions

Preset the the oven to 350 and gently spray an 8×8 baking dish with canola oil. Combine the first a few ingredients together in a sizable bowl. Combine the water with the nut butter, Liquid Smoke, and soy sauce and add it to the dry ingredients. Mix to mix well after which knead gently in the bowl 15-60 seconds (the significantly less you knead this, the greater tender that is; the much longer, the chewier).

Set the dough in the baking dish and flatten it to ensure that it evenly fills the pan. Have a sharp knife and is not the best way to go in to 8 strips; after that turn the pan and cut those whitening strips in half to create 16 pieces:

Input it in the the oven and bake intended for 25 minutes. Although it's cooking make your grill.

Remove it from the oven and cautiously re-cut each tape, discussing each lower to make certain that the ribz pull aside easily later. Generously brush the top with barbecue sauce. Have it for the grill and invert the whole baking dish onto the barbeque (or use a large spatula to lift up the seitan out, positioning it sauce-side down on the grill). Brush the top from the seitan with more spices:

Watch it carefully to be sure that it doesn't burn. Once it's sufficiently brown using one side, change over and make the other part, increasing the sauce, in the event necessary. When completed, remove to a plate and cut or perhaps pull apart the individual ribs to
to serve.

Barbecued Style Braised Short Ribs Recipe

Ingredients

2 tablespoons vegetable oil
5 pounds lean beef short ribs, cut into 3-inch pieces
1 teaspoon salt
1/2 teaspoon fresh ground black pepper
1 large onion, cut into thick slices and separated into rings
5 carrot, (7-1/2")s carrots, peeled and cut into chunks
4 cloves garlic, coarsely chopped
1 (16-ounce) can tomato sauce
1 cup barbeque sauces
1 cup beef broth

Directions

Step one Preheat oven to 325 degrees Farreneheit (165 degrees C). Advertisement
Step a couple of Heat oil more than medium heat in a large, large, oven-safe pot or Dutch oven, and brown

the ribs on the sides, regarding 5 minutes, employed in batches if important. Sprinkle ribs with salt and black pepper as they will brown. Transfer prepared ribs to newspaper towels to mark up extra essential oil.

Step 3 Mix the onion jewelry and carrots in to the same weed, and cook and stir before the onions turn translucent and start to brown, regarding 8 minutes. Mix in the garlic herb, and cook until fragrant, about one particular more minute. Mix in tomato sauce, cooking area sauce, and meat broth; bring the sauce to a boil, and simmer for 1 minute to blend flavours. Stir in the browned ribs.

Step four Cover the pot, and bake in the preheated oven until the rib various meats is very soft, about 2 1/2 hours. Turn the ribs occasionally although cooking. Season to taste with salt and black self defense before serving sizzling.

BBQ Baby Back Ribs

Ingredients

2 tablespoons light brown sugar
1 tablespoon dry mustard
1 tablespoon paprika
1 teaspoon smoked paprika
1 teaspoon freshly ground black pepper
1 teaspoon garlic salt
2 racks baby back pork ribs (4 pounds)
jamie's bbq sauce, recipe follows
1 tablespoon canola oil
2 tablespoons finely chopped onions
2 cups apple cider vinegar
1 1/2 cups ketchup
3/4 cup light brown sugar
3 tablespoons dijon mustard
1 tablespoon Worcestershire sauce
2 teaspoons chili powder
1 teaspoon cayenne pepper
kosher salt and freshly ground black pepper

Directions

Preset the the oven to 350 degrees Farrenheit.

Mix together the brown sugar, mustard, paprika, smoked paprika, black pepper and garlic salt collectively in a small bowl. Be sure to separation any lumps together with your fingers. Reserve one particular tablespoon of rub in a tiny bowl for offering.

Remove the sterling silver skin from the underside of the ribs by slipping your fingers beneath the thin membrane and pulling that off. Repeat with the second rack. Stroke the ribs together with the seasoning on both sides. Place in a single layer in a large cooking pan and covers tightly with heavy-duty foil. Place the roasting pan in to the oven and bake before the ribs are tender, regarding 1 hour 15 minutes.

Preheat the grill to medium heat.

Grill the steak on each part for 15 moments, watching and flipping when necessary, intended for 30 minutes total. Baste with Jamie's BBQ Sauce the last 10 minutes. (The sauce continues on at the end since it is sugar based and you don't want to burn your steak.)

Let the racks rest 5 minutes before slicing into individual steak. Sprinkle the lower ribs with the reserved dry scrub and serve along with extra marinade.

Heat the olive oil in a medium saucepan over medium-high temperature. Add the onions and stir until softened. Add the vinegar, ketchup, dark brown sugar, mustard, Worcestershire sauce, chili dust, cayenne pepper and some salt and dark pepper to the saucepan and simmer on medium-low heat until thickened, regarding 35 minutes.

BBQ Boneless Country Ribs

Ingredients

3 4 pounds 3-4 boneless pork country-style ribs
2 tablespoons olive oil
1/2 teaspoon seasoned salt
1/2 large onion, sliced
1 1/2 cups water
1 cup ketchup
1/4 cup Worcestershire sauce
1 teaspoon chili powder
2 dashes red pepper sauces

Directions

Preheat oven to 425°F. Coat bottom of baking dish with 1 tea spoon of olive olive oil. Place ribs in dish, separating all of them slightly. Drizzle left over 1 tablespoon olive oil over leading of ribs and rub to coating. Sprinkle seasoned sodium lightly overall. Place sliced onions about top of steak. Roast ribs for 425°F for 40 minutes.

2 In the meantime, in medium saucepan over medium temperature, combine water, ketchup, Worcestershire sauce, soup powder and red pepper sauce. Provide boil. Reduce heat to low and continue to simmer sauce until that is reduced and thickened a lttle bit.

three or more After thirty minutes of roasting, pour BBQ GRILL sauce over steak, reserving about 1 cup for later. Reduce oven temp to 350°F and bake ribs one more 1 hr (or longer, according to thickness of ribs), basting with sauce every 12-15 minutes. Ribs will be done when meats is tender and cooked through, and the internal temperature reaches a minimum of 145°F. You are able to covers the pan usually with foil to get the final 30 minutes of making cookies if the steak appear to become drying out. Make sure you keep basting the meat frequently to continue to keep it moist and delicious.

4 Transfer steak to a plate and pour BBQ sauce over most. Serve immediately.

BBQ Pulled Pork Sandwiches

Ingredients

3 1/2 pounds roughly 3-1/2 (1.5kg) boston butt
1 tablespoon (13g) brown sugar
1 tablespoon (7g) garlic powder
1 tablespoon (7g) mustard powder
2 1/2 to 3 2-1/2 to 3 tbs (18g-22g)paprika
8 buns
bbq sauce
1 package coleslaw
1 bottle of litehouse bleu cheese vinaigrette

Directions

Mix the dry ingredients together.
Rub the dry mixture on the meat, coating all sides.
Place the meat in a roasting pan.
Cover the meat with plastic wrap and invite it rest in the refrigerator, preferably overnight.

When you are ready to cook the meat, take away the plastic wrap and cover the pan tightly with foil.

Bake the meat at 275 degrees before internal temperature of the roast is 200 degrees and the meat pulls as well as the bone. The cook time changes based on the size of the roast. The entire guideline is that it will require 1 - 1 1/2 hours for every and every pound of meat. (If you utilize a glass pan, place the cold pan in the cold oven and let them heat together to prevent your pan from cracking.)

Following the first three hours baste the meat using its juices every hour.

Get rid of the meat from the oven and invite it rest for 15 minutes.

Shred the meat into pieces with a fork.

Toss the coleslaw and the dressing, mixing in the dressing to taste.

Assemble the sandwiches, spooning pulled pork on underneath portion of the bun, drizzling it with sauce and topping it with coleslaw.

Best Barbecue Ribs Ever

Ingredients

1/4 cup brown sugar
2 tablespoons chili powder
kosher salt and freshly ground black pepper
1 teaspoon dried oregano
1/2 teaspoon cayenne pepper
1/2 teaspoon garlic powder
1/2 teaspoon onion powder
2 racks baby back ribs
1 cup low-sodium chicken broth
2 tablespoons apple cider vinegar
1 cup barbecue sauce

Directions

Combine the brown sugar, chili powder, 1 tablespoon salt, 1 teaspoon black pepper, the oregano, cayenne, garlic powder and onion powder in a little bowl and rub the mixture on both sides of the ribs. Cover and refrigerate 1 hour or overnight.

Preheat the oven to 250 degrees F. In a roasting pan, combine the broth and vinegar. Add the ribs to the pan. Cover with foil and tightly seal. Bake 2 hours. Remove the ribs from the pan and place them on a platter. Pour the liquid from the pan right into a saucepan and bring to a boil. Lower heat to a simmer and cook until reduced by half. Add the barbecue sauce.

Preheat a patio grill to medium high. Put the ribs on the grill and cook about 5 minutes on each side, until browned and slightly charred. Slice the ribs between your bones and toss them in a big bowl with the sauce. Serve hot.

Best Darn Instant Pot Boneless Pork Chops

Ingredients

2 pork chops, boneless 1" thick
2 tablespoons brown sugar
1 teaspoon salt
1 teaspoon black pepper
1 teaspoon paprika
1/2 teaspoon onion powder
1 tablespoon butter
1 cup chicken broth
1/2 tablespoon Worcestershire sauce
1 teaspoon liquid smoke

Directions

1) Mix spices and brown sugar and rub into both sides of pork chops.
2) Set Instant Pot on saute (high) and add tablespoon butter. Once hot, add pork chops and brown on both sides for 1-2 minutes each. Remove pork chops and reserve. Press cancel.
3) Add 1 cup chicken broth and use a wooden spoon to deglaze the bits off underneath of the pot. Add

Worcestershire sauce and liquid smoke and add pork chops to the pot in the liquid.

4) Secure lid, make certain vent is defined to "sealing" and pressure cook (manual) for 7 minutes. When done, allow pressure to naturally release for 12 minutes. After 12 minutes, quick release others, remove lid and pork chops.

5) Let pork chops rest for about five minutes before serving.

I've tried several pork chop recipes in as soon as Pot but honestly, have only had mediocre results. THEREFORE I set out to make an effort to make pork chops how they need to be - browned externally, juicy and delicious inside. Sounds simple enough, right? Well after twelve roughly attempts, i've finally got down a perfect recipe.

I've found the most effective boneless pork chops for the moment Pot are one inch thick. Not only are they easy to come across at the supermarket, however they simply would be the best thickness for pressure cooking.

Start with an easy seasoning on both sides of the pork chops of salt, pepper, onion powder, paprika and brown sugar. Then, using your Instant Pot setting on saute (high), melt a tablespoon of butter. When it's good and hot, add the pork chops and brown each side for approximately 1-2 minutes. That brown sugar may char a bit, but that's ok. After the pork chops undoubtedly are a beautiful golden brown, remove from the pot and set on a plate. Press cancel in order to avoid the saute mode and add 1 cup of chicken broth to the pot. Use a wooden spoon to "deglaze" underneath of the pot. This is simply scraping all of the bits off underneath. Then, add the Worcestershire sauce and Liquid Smoke. Add the pork chops to the liquid, secure the lid, close the seal and pressure cook for 7 minutes. When cycle is complete let naturally release for 12 minutes. Remove from pot and let rest for approximately.

Best-Ever Barbecued Ribs

Ingredients

2 1/2 tablespoons kosher salt
1 tablespoon dry mustard
1 tablespoon paprika
1/2 teaspoon cayenne pepper
1/2 teaspoon freshly ground black pepper
8 pounds baby back pork ribs (8 racks) or st. louis-style spareribs (4 racks)
low-salt chicken broth (optional)
1 1/2 cups store-bought or homemade barbecue sauces plus more

Directions

Preheat oven to 300°. Combine first 5 ingredients in a little bowl. Place each rack of ribs on a double layer of foil; sprinkle rub around ribs. Wrap racks individually and divide between 2 baking sheets.
Bake ribs until very tender but not falling apart, about 2 hours for baby backs and 3 hours for spareribs. Carefully unwrap ribs; pour any juices from foil into a 4-

cup heatproof measuring cup; reserve juices. Let ribs cool completely. DO AHEAD: Ribs can be baked up to 3 days ahead (the flavor could be more developed, and the cold ribs will hold together better on the grill because they heat through). Cover and chill juices. Rewrap ribs in foil and chill.

Build a medium-hot fire in a charcoal grill, or heat a gas grill to high. Add broth or water to rib juices, if needed, to measure 1 1/2 cups. Whisk in barbecue sauce to blend.

Grill ribs, basting with barbecue sauce mixture and turning frequently, until lacquered and charred in places and heated through, 7-10 minutes. Transfer to a cutting board; cut between ribs to split up. Transfer to a platter and serve with additional barbecue sauce.

Beth's Melt in Your Mouth Barbecue Ribs

Ingredients

4 pounds pork ribs
3/4 cup light brown sugar
1 teaspoon hickory smoke salt
1 tablespoon garlic powder
1 tablespoon paprika
1/2 teaspoon ground red pepper (optional)
2 cups favorite bbq sauces

Directions

1. Preheat oven to 300 degrees f.
2. Peel off tough membrane that covers the bony side of the ribs.
3. Mix together the sugar and spices to make the rub.
4. Apply rub to ribs on all sides.
5. Lay ribs on two layers of foil, shiny side out and meaty side down.
6. Lay two layers of foil along with ribs and roll and crimp edges tightly, edges facing up to seal.

7. Put on baking sheet and bake for 2-2 1/2 hours or until meat is starting to shrink away from the ends of the bone.
8. Remove from oven.
9. Heat broiler.
10. Cut ribs into serving sized portions of 2 or 3 3 ribs.
11. Arrange on broiler pan, bony side up.
12. Brush on sauce.
13. Broil for 1 or 2 2 minutes until sauce is cooked on and bubbly.
14. Turn ribs over.
15. Repeat on other side.
16. Alternately, you can grill the ribs on your grill to cook on the sauce.

Chipotle Barbecue Ribs

Ingredients

2 racks baby back ribs (about 3 1/2 pounds each)
1 tablespoon paprika
1 tablespoon garlic powder
kosher salt and freshly ground black pepper
2 tablespoons vegetable oil
1 medium onion, chopped
kosher salt
2 cloves garlic, finely chopped
1 1/2 cups no-sugar-added ketchup
3/4 cup fresh orange juice
2 teaspoons Worcestershire sauce
2 chipotles in adobo, chopped, plus 1 tablespoon adobo sauces

Directions

For the ribs: Preheat the oven to 350 degrees F. Line a huge rimmed baking pan with foil.

Place the ribs on the prepared baking pan meat-side up. Sprinkle them with the paprika, garlic powder, 1 tablespoon salt and a generous amount of pepper. Rub the spices all around the ribs.

Cover the pan tightly with foil and bake before meat is quite tender and can certainly be pulled off the bone, about 2 hours.

For the barbecue sauce: Meanwhile, heat the oil in a medium saucepan over medium heat. Add the onions and 1/2 teaspoon salt and cook, stirring often, until very soft and golden brown, about 20 minutes. Add the garlic and cook, stirring, 1 minute. Add the ketchup, orange juice, Worcestershire, chipotles and adobo and 1/2 cup water. Raise the heat to bring to a boil, then decrease the heat to keep at a simmer until slightly thickened, about ten minutes. Transfer to a blender and puree until smooth (be cautious when blending hot liquids). Alternately, an immersion blender can be utilized in the pot.

Finish the ribs: Preheat the grill to medium-high (or set the oven to broil).

Reserve in regards to a cup of the barbecue sauce for serving alongside the ribs. Brush a small amount of the remaining sauce on the bone side of the ribs and a generous amount on the meaty side.

Grill the ribs, meaty-side up, before underside is lightly charred, about three minutes. Turn the ribs over and grill until the meaty side is charred in spots, three to five five minutes (if using the oven, simply broil for three to five five minutes). Transfer to a cutting board and cut each rack in two. Serve immediately with the reserved sauce privately.

Fall-Off-The-Bone Oven Baked Ribs Recipe

Ingredients

2 to 2 1/2 pounds baby back pork ribs
salt and black pepper
1 tablespoon olive oil
1/4 cup finely diced onions
1/2 teaspoon ground cumin
1/2 cup ketchup, try our homemade ketchup recipe
1 tablespoon hot chili sauce (suggestion sriracha)
2 tablespoons light brown sugar
1 tablespoon apple cider vinegar
salt and ground pepper, to taste

Directions

Heat oven to 275 degrees Fahrenheit (135C).

If the ribs still have the thin membrane covering the back of the rack, take it off. Observe how in the notes section below.

Season both sides of the ribs with a generous amount of salt and pepper then place, meat-side up, into a sizable roasting pan or rimmed baking sheet. (It might be necessary to slice the ribs in half in order for them to fit in to the pan).

Cover the pan or baking sheet tightly with aluminum foil, and bake before meat falls easily from the bones, 3 to 4 4 hours.

As the ribs bake, make the barbecue sauce. Heat the essential olive oil in a saucepan over medium heat.

Add the onions and cook until soft and translucent, 5 to 8 minutes. Stir in the cumin and cook for an additional 30 seconds.

Add the ketchup, hot chili sauce, brown sugar, and apple cider vinegar. Stir to mix, season with salt then cook for 2 minutes. Set aside in preparation for the ribs to complete roasting.

Take away the ribs from the oven, discard the aluminum foil and generously brush both sides with barbecue sauce.

Optional: Move an oven rack near the the surface of the oven. Turn broiler to high and broil the ribs for 3-4 minutes, just until the barbecue sauce begins to caramelize. (Keep a close eye on the ribs while they broil so they the sauce does not burn.)

www.ingramcontent.com/pod-product-compliance
Lightning Source LLC
Chambersburg PA
CBHW071440070526
44578CB00001B/160